THE DILEMMA
OF CARING

THE DILEMMA
OF CARING

For Your Older Loved One or Friend

By

ELIZABETH GILMAN McNULTY

and

MERYL S. DANN

Chicago, Illinois

CHARLES C THOMAS • PUBLISHER
Springfield • Illinois • U.S.A.

12 - 8 - 92

Published and Distributed Throughout the World by
CHARLES C THOMAS • PUBLISHER
2600 South First Street
Springfield, Illinois 62717

© *1985 by* CHARLES C THOMAS • PUBLISHER
ISBN 0-398-05159-3
Library of Congress Catalog Card Number: 85-12517

With THOMAS BOOKS *careful attention is given to all details of manufacturing
and design. It is the Publisher's desire to present books that are satisfactory as to their
physical qualities and artistic possibilities and appropriate for their particular use.*
THOMAS BOOKS *will be true to those laws of quality that assure a good name
and good will.*

Printed in the United States of America
Q-R-3

Library of Congress Cataloging in Publication Data

McNulty, Elizabeth G.
  The dilemma of caring.

  1. Aged--Home care--United States--Case studies.
2. Aged--Care and hygiene--United States--Case studies.
3. Aged--United States--Family relationships--Case
studies. I. Dann, Meryl S. II. Title.
HV1461.M39 1985   305.2'6'0973   85-12517
ISBN 0-398-05159-3

This book is lovingly dedicated to our parents,
George and Sydne Dann
and
Alvin and Leah Gilman.

PREFACE

A T THE TURN of this century, 10 percent of the population of the United States was over 55 years of age. Some eight decades later, that number has increased to over 20 percent. And, given current projections, the number of people in the over 55 age group is expected to increase to 33 percent during the next 50 years.

Fifty years from now, one out of three persons in this country will be over 55, one out of four over 65, and one out of eight over 75. As Americans move into these older age groups, acute health problems give way to chronic conditions — conditions that currently limit the activities of 50 percent of the over 75 age group, 22 percent to the point at which the person can no longer carry on a major life activity, becoming dependent on persons or equipment aids.

Although older people today have fewer mental problems than people in younger age groups, they are most often afflicted with cognitive impairment (more commonly referred to as senility) — the reason that many older persons are not able to live by themselves. It is also the principle reason for the institutionalization of older persons.

Finances notwithstanding, living arrangements for these persons depend, basically, on the extent of their need for help with personal care or home management or both. Living arrangements run the gamut from living alone to institutionalization, with intermediate arrangements such as living with a family member or friend or living in independent groups or retirement complexes.

What impact will the graying of America have on individuals, family members, and friends? Given no startling changes in current trends, just about every family in the United States will face — at some point in time — the dilemma of caring for an older loved one, family member or friend. It's a responsibility with far-reaching physical, emotional, financial, and social ramifications for everyone involved.

These are the hard facts of the matter. But what are the human realities of life for and with the older person in this country? It is hoped that useful insights will be found in this book, which is about the human equation of growing old in America.

ACKNOWLEDGMENTS

WE GRATEFULLY acknowledge the contributions of the countless people who openly and sensitively told their stories in hopes of helping millions of others going through similar experiences. Special appreciation also goes to all those who gave us help, support, and advice and to those who've asked where to buy the book, reaffirming our belief it was one that had to be written. Finally, our thanks to the publisher for his patience.

CONTENTS

THE DILEMMA
OF CARING

1.

THE DILEMMA

"THE OLD MAN is driving me crazy!" "If I could just have a little peace!" "I can't stand to be in the same room with her!" "He's destroying my family!" "I wish she were dead! Oh why doesn't she just go ahead and die?"

For every despairing person who has uttered these words about a sick or senile loved one, there are thousands more who have thought them — over and over and over again. But, too often, feelings of guilt, shame, and responsibility stifle honest reaction to these painful situations, blurring the fine line between responsible caring and unreasonable sacrifice — of self or family.

Few people alive today will be spared the dilemma of caring for an older loved one. And in the changing times in which we live, the care of an elderly person most often becomes a matter of the most viable option, not the perfect solution. In this book, you will meet twelve very different people — all with one thing in common: responsibility of caring for a person who can no longer care for himself. In the pages that follow, these individuals share their own search for that viable option. They describe the situations in which they found themselves, the feelings they had about them, the factors that affected their decisions concerning the care of the older person, and a retrospective of their own personal dilemmas. Their words reflect the inner, intense, and complex emotions of persons intimately

3

involved in caring for another person.

The people who tell their stories here come from a variety of backgrounds — educational, occupational, economic, cultural, and religious. You will read in these pages the story of a domestic worker, a photographer, a businessman, a carpenter, a woman executive, an engineer, a manicurist, an ice skater and her policeman husband, a social worker, a dancer, an administrator. These men and women represent a rich cross section of national and ethnic backgrounds. They are from different racial backgrounds — Caucasian, Asian, and Black — and religious affiliations — Catholic, Protestant, Jewish, and Buddhist. Indirectly, you will meet other people, whose words are echoed here, helping to form the fabric of this book.

Each of these people* brings to his personal situation the life experiences that have molded his thoughts, beliefs, and behaviors. Perhaps you will identify with one or more of these men and women, gaining insight and understanding from the decisions each made — the initial decisions and decisions made as conditions and situations changed.

For Martin Ewing and Tom Hannon, clear-cut options were available. Though the settings were different — one urban and one rural — Martin and Tom had the same viable choices to make. But Martins pact with his sister dictated his decision — a decision that, fortunately, was economically possible. Martin arranged for his parents to be cared for in their own home. Tom and his sisters tried that, too. But it didn't work for long, because no live-in companion was available, no matter how hard Tom and his sisters tried to find one. Their answer, finally, was a nursing home.

The childhood experiences of Carol and Ed Kallish made predictable their decision to care for Carol's mother — a victim of Alzheimer's disease — in their high rise apartment. Together — and with the help of their housekeeper — they cared

---

*When it has been the person's preference, identifying references have been changed.

for Carol's mother, watching helplessly as she deteriorated over the two-year period.

Helping her stepfather care for her mother, from a distance of 150 miles, kept Mae Johnson on the road — by car or bus — for the last years of her mother's life, even during the illness and hospitalization of her own husband. For the last six months, Mae stayed in the family home, caring for her mother there or overseeing her care as she moved in and out of hospitals and nursing homes.

Together, Pat Hughes and her brother made decisions — from a distance — about their aging and increasingly senile mother. Their hope was to keep her in the family home. And for years, they were able to do that with the help of a home health agency. Finally, the two realized that a time would come when their mother was no longer able to stay in her house, and a nursing home would be the only answer.

An only child, Marty took her mother into her own home after she had been institutionalized as the result of a stroke. This was to be a temporary arrangement only, made necessary by the high cost of convalescent care. But Marty's mother didn't want to go back to her own home and so, the arrangement became long-term, if not permanent.

Joan Bradley's husband and his sister tried everything they could think of to keep their mother from going into a nursing home. When she could no longer live alone, she moved into Joan and Don's home. But when that didn't work, Joan's mother-in-law moved into a townhouse in a retirement community — until she got sick. And then she was no longer welcome in the retirement community and a nursing home was the only other alternative.

With plenty of room in her own home, Leah Goldman brought her mother to live with her and her husband, at the time her mother could no longer live alone in her New York apartment. Although retirement hotels were considered, Leah's mother stayed with her for several years, going regularly to a day care program for part of that time. Finally, when Leah could no longer cope with the situation in her home, she put her mother in a nursing home, and continues the painful visiting to this day.

When Flo Jackson's mother-in-law paid Flo and her husband a somewhat unexpected visit, she moved in bag and baggage. A semi-invalid at the time she came, the woman's condition steadily worsened. But due to the family's economic situation — Flo's husband could no longer work, and there were small children to raise — and their fear of nursing homes, Flo chose to care for her mother-in-law herself. And she gave 13 years of her life to it — years that took a great physical and emotional toll. She did it without any help from anyone, particularly from her husband's family.

For Gigi Matsubara, the Nisei wife of a native-born Japanese, there was no question about what her decision would be. When her husband became terminally ill on a visit to his homeland, Gigi gave up her job, packed or sold their belongings — for the second time in their 33-year marriage — and moved with him to Japan to be with him during the last year of his life. There was no dilemma — only sadness — for Gigi in caring for her loved one.

Making decisions for a non-family member caused dilemmas of another kind for James Walters who became the legal guardian of his wife's long-time friend. The woman's only sister — an invalid, who lived a half-a-continent away — was not able to take Edna into her home. Because the woman was alone and could not manage for herself, her friend and her friend's husband took over Edna's care and the management of her estate, all at the mercy of lawyers and judges, many of whom seemed to have little concern for the central figure — the aging loved one.

Jane Stanhope was one of a network of devoted former students who helped care for two aging ballet dancers in their small apartment. Each member of the network had an important supporting role, but major decisions were made by the lawyer member of the group. Since neither of the old gentlemen had any close family, their care was solely in the hands of their nurses and 15 loving friends.

For each person in this book, caring for the loved one in his own surroundings was the hoped-for solution. For most of them — because of financial, emotional, or societal reasons or because of lack of information — a nursing home was the solution of last resort. During the course of events described in these pages, only Martin, Gigi, and Jane and her friends were able to keep their loved ones in their own surroundings until the end — or until a final hospitalization. Flo and Marty, trapped by circumstance, cared for their loved ones in their own homes. In each case, it was an entrapment that had far-reaching repercussions on the person and her family. As conditions and situations changed, the other people you will encounter here looked to as many other resources as they knew were available — day care centers, home health agencies, convalescent homes, rehabilitation centers — in hopes of delaying or making unnecessary — the inevitable admission of their loved one to a nursing home.

Each of the people in this book did the best he knew how — with the resources available and the knowledge he had — out of love and caring concern for another person. And most have no regrets.

What would *you* do, if you found yourself in one of the situations described in the following pages?

2.

THE PEOPLE AND THEIR STORIES

OH, THOSE AWFUL SIGNS

HAVING BEEN TOLD that their mother was already showing signs of senility and would become a handful after the death of their father, Tom Hannon and his two sisters started looking at their options. Although a number of options were available to them, Tom wonders whether the pressures of time, distance, and those "awful signs" caused them to make a premature decision.

This is the story of the Hannon family's search for the most viable option and of Tom's feelings eight years after the fact.

Mother was 80, maybe 81, when my father died. Just before he died, the family doctor said, "Once your father's gone, your mother is really going to be a handful. She's already showing the signs of senility and other disabilities of old age." And with that, we — my two sisters and I — already had the doctor's ominous input firmly implanted in our brains.

The older you are, the normal built-in rehabilitation process that every widow or widower is supposed to have doesn't function too well. At age 81, you aren't going to have the kind of recovery that a person in his 60s is going to have. Even though we knew this, whenever this sign or that sign showed up, why it was a mark against mother. And now at this stage of the game — many years later — I'm inclined to think that we made our moves a little quicker than we ideally would have. Distance has a way of prompting things like that. (My sister, Avis, and I are more than 300 miles away from the home town and my sister, Mary Ann, is more than 1,000.)

Mother was always difficult, but she was a lot more difficult after dad died. One minute she would be very independent, and the next she would be crying for help. She kept the car and continued to drive for a while — much to the dismay of the local authorities and of every mother with a child under five. (You weren't too sure that mother was going to stay on the street.) Finally, she surrendered her driver's license. The time came for her driver's license exam and she failed the driving test. After her second test, the examiner said, "Either I'm going to resign or Mrs. Hannon is going to turn in her driver's license." He was more or less on the verge of a heart attack or a stroke, whichever was going to come first.

Losing her driver's license made mother increasingly helpless. Wheels are very important in a town of 600 people. There's no public transportation. And in Clifton there really was no organization for senior citizens — for local wheeling around. So she had to make arrangements with friends to take her here or take her there. Since mother was so used to being independent, she really didn't do too well on that score. Come to think of it, there *was* one organization that did have a school bus or something like that set up. But mother wasn't going to use that. It was too inconvenient, because she had to walk a ways to get the bus. She never really had used public transportation, except during the war — to take a bus from a bus station to a bus station. She wasn't really able to convert from private transportation to public transportation.

In the months after dad died, it was "Yes, I'm going to take care of myself," then "No, I can't do that." This was a source of constant frustration to us. If one of us had lived next door, things would probably have happened differently. Most likely, mother would have gone to a nursing home at some point in time, but not as soon as she did. The distance, her age, and the turmoil of the recent loss precipitated the actions we took — as did those ever-present *signs*.

None of the three of us — my sisters and I — feel that life should be dominated by the older generation. And I don't feel that life should be dominated by the youngest generation either. But if a decision is going to have to be made, you're going to make it in favor of the youngest generation.

Mother was a very important part of our responsibility and held an important place in our hearts. Even so, we just had to take care of things in a logical fashion. But even logic, in my feeling, was really superceded by the pressures of distance.

Physically, mother was in pretty good condition. She had most of her faculties. You worry, of course, about things like incontinence. And she did have a few accidents. But, heck, it could be just a case of the flu. When something like that would happen, we'd think, "Oh, oh! *This is another sign. Look out for this sign!*" Really, this sign business is a bad thing. This preconditioning isn't the nicest thing. The signs always show up before it's absolutely necessary to make the move. I think it's nice if you can extend the time that the person has in his own home — if that's important to him.

If you're going to be preconditioned, the source of the preconditioning should be someone else who's gone down the same road. Not your family doctor. He's giving you technical and clinical information from his objective experience. And my feeling is that objectivity tends to be a little too mechanical, a little too clincial. The doctor's advice is a good guideline, but nothing more.

If one of your high school buddies says, "My mother has the same problem, and I don't really know what I'm going to do with her either," you'll find you can help each other. Maybe another buddy will say, "Well my mother, bless her heart, has gone this route. And here's what we did. And here are some of the mistakes we made." And another one might say, "I really feel terrible about what I did." And you're probably going to say to yourself, "She's just on a guilt trip. She probably did the right thing, but she hasn't settled it in her own mind yet." I suppose that helping someone else feel better about his situation makes you feel better too. But I think this is only a by-product. You're thinking about yourself at this particular stage, because this is a very serious thing.

After my father died, my mother stayed in the house on the farm for at the most two years — maybe just a year. She lived alone. We tried to get her a live-in housekeeper, as a matter of fact. We finally lined up a lady from the state capital, which was 30 miles away. She came to visit mother, and she talked to a few of the local citizens. Then she packed up and left the next day. I wasn't exactly sure what that meant, but that's the way it worked out. Well, mother wasn't really very receptive to the idea anyway, which probably helped the candidate change her mind.

When my grandmother was in her last years, she had a live-in companion/housekeeper, Mrs. Webb. She was a lady who was maybe five or ten years younger than my grandmother. She took care of different things and she would stay overnight maybe three or four days a week. The rest of the time Mrs. Webb would go back to her own house. She really didn't want to move in with my grandmother and call that her home.

My sisters and I thought that if we could find someone like Mrs. Webb, it would be just fine. But we couldn't do that. It's more difficult now than it was then, what with social security and the various pension plans available. Now, when you're 65 or 70, you just adjust to living on the cash available. There's not much reason to go out and earn any more, so there are not many people available.

During these months, we did all of the decision making, all of the errands, all of the paper work, and all of the reports on the farm. Legally, though, mother still had some connection with the farm — for a year or two. Having some small responsibility for the farm gave her some connection with the real world, even though she couldn't really handle it.

Mother would sometimes neglect to pay the bills. She would pay no bills, as a matter of fact. Someone from the telephone company would call us and say, "Gee, somebody's going to have to pay the telephone bill." Being a small town, the telephone manager was a classmate of my sister, Avis, so he'd call up and say, "Avis, somebody's going to have to pay the phone bill." "Okay, we'll take care of it." Then we'd check and find that, probably, the light bill and the water bill hadn't been paid either. So we finally took over all of the bill paying and she really was relieved of all her duties. But mother was still living in the house. She would get all the bills and would complain about them — rightfully or wrongfully — but at least she felt some involvement. The bills were always too high. She'd say, "That's an awful price to have to pay." Looking back, I guess it *was* an outrage compared to what she remembered paying. She couldn't keep up with the changes.

Mother was also getting pretty careless about cooking, cleaning, and shopping, which worried us a little. The fact that she had a gas stove also worried us. And sometimes she would leave the water running in the kitchen and it would get to the top of the sink and overflow onto the kitchen floor. I could do the same stunt and get away with it. But if you're 80 years old and pull that stunt, *you're in trouble!*

Now paying attention to these signs is not out of line. Signs are useful and they help you make a decision. But you had better not rely on them completely, or you're going to feel a degree of regret later on. I'm not saying that I really feel reget — at least I don't now. I sort of feel that we were trapped into making an early decision. We were trapped by distance. We were trapped by the facts as they were — that we were never able to make that stop-gap move of getting someone to stay with her, never able to overcome her built-in stubbornness. Mother would never go along with anything we thought would extend her time in her own home.

During these months, mother would call each of us and say things like, "You don't call me often enough," when someone had called her just the day before. "The renter on the farm is robbing us blind. You don't care what's going on out here. You're just taking care of yourself and your kids. You don't care about me." (Forgetfulness and paranoia — *more signs!*) The three of us got chewed out equally — at different times. There would be one angel and two devils — always one angel. But the roles changed. We each played all the parts.

We got so used to hearing her yell at us that it wasn't hard to yell back. It worked out real good. "No mother, that isn't gonna work," "No mother, that's a bad idea." Then she'd moan and cry and tell us to go to hell. I would just yell back at her or slam the receiver down. Then the telephone would ring again inside of a minute and she'd apologize. I'd say, "Fine, but let's not talk about it right now. Let's not talk about anything else, either, because there's no other way we can talk but to scream. Call me back in a day or two." She'd call back in five minutes and I'd pick up the telephone and say, "Not now!"

There were times when I would be pretty upset by the telephone calls. But it was going on so regularly that finally I got a bit calloused to the whole thing. It was still upsetting because I knew that all of the little things, all of the little faults you have at 45 or 50 are magnified when you hit 80. You're more fixed in your ways. If you're a little obnoxious earlier on, you're a hardliner at 80.

I regret that we could not have set up a smoother road for mother. But we just couldn't overcome the barriers. The logistics were hell, pure hell. First, as far as getting someone to live with her, we tried and tried and simply couldn't get the job done. Secondly, we couldn't get any cooperation from my mother.

It took us about a year-and-a-half to make our final moves. First, you make a list of options — some of which you are going to consider, some of which you are going to reject — living in one of our homes, for instance. We rejected that idea because it would have been an imposition on the rest of our families. As I say, the oldest generation is to be treated with respect, love, and care, but like with the youngest generation, you have to remain in control of your own life. My mother was one of those dominant personalities. And there was no way that any of the three of us could have had her in our homes — without breaking her, or us. And I didn't want either to happen. I didn't want to break her spirit.

Also, I don't think there would have been any great advantage for her to make the move to Arizona or Springfield — far from Clifton. She was a lifetime resident of Will County. Now mother *thought* she would like to live with one of us — any one of the three of us. Some people could make that move, but I really don't think my mother could have. Since she still had spirit, we couldn't make a cage for her in one of our homes. That's no deal either.

There were other options. We thought of the British Home, where Mary's father spent his last years. It was an awfully nice retirement home. It was full service, from walk-in type care to care of residents in the infirmary or in a hospital in their final, dying days. Everything was handled right there; handled with dignity. We thought this would be an alternative for my mother.

We also had located apartment facilities in the suburb next to ours. There she would have had her own car, in the parking lot, even though she couldn't drive it. In this urban location, we could have found someone to take her for a ride in her own car. So we tried the apartment approach. Mother was in on a visit and I had her take a look at one of the apartments. And it was "very nice" *but* . . . . . . so that took care of that.

Regardless of what her answers were — which were all negative answers — it didn't make any difference. You couldn't win that argument because she was right. "Why do I want to leave my nice place in Clifton? Everything works there. And I've got my people there." The real truth was that she couldn't be taken out of Will County. She couldn't take the transplant. She really couldn't have moved into our house after all. So we had to scrap all three of those options.

At about this time, we were right up against the wall. Mother could not stay in her house alone any longer. If we couldn't get anyone in there, she would have to move. Or else, which might have been just as humane, we would have to let her stay there and perish. Those were our choices. There was a county nurses organization in the area. We had a nurse from there for my father and it worked out fine then. But we were advised not to have one of these nurses for my mother, because my mother's care requirements were greater. It seemed to us, then, that the smart thing for us to say was, "Let's just take mother and trot her off to a nursing home."

We had started looking at nursing homes about six months after my father died. For those first six months, we thought mother might be able to make it at home. At the time, Avis really had very negative feelings about nursing homes. But after six months of exposure to the way things would be if we didn't do something, we all changed our opinions.

There were three nursing homes that we could choose from. The Will County Hospital has nursing home facilities, and it was in the county seat, which was almost a home town to mother. Plainfield and Clifton, which were seven miles apart, was her area. Will County Hospital would have been good. You had to go on a waiting list, but we were lining things up so we could have gotten her in there. Then there was Atkins, which was a private nursing home. It was also very nice — kind of a country club type. There were a few local citizens at Atkins. Finally, there was Zenon, where we took her. We went from A to Z — Atkins to Zenon.

We chose Zenon because we liked it the best. It was the best. It wasn't a country club as Atkins was. Its price was higher than Will County, but not measurably higher. And there were some people there from Monroe, which was mother's birthplace and where she lived in her childhood — in fact, up until she was married. So Zenon really was the most practical choice. And, physically, it was the best plant.

At Zenon, the floors were sparkling. The place never smelled. And they were always doing the laundry. It was a clean place. Neat and clean, not clinical. There were posters on the walls. It looked a little bit like kindergarten, which was a bit of an insult to someone just coming in — the kindergarten air about it. "Mamie, we're going to have a birthday party for you and we're going to put on our party hats and have a good time." It's a little kindergarteny, but that's as far as it went. It wasn't really heavy. It's a little insulting, though, to think that your mother's going back to kindergarten. In fact, she is. And maybe the sooner you get that into your head, the better off you'll be.

When it came time to take mother to the home, my two sisters and I went out there. Mother had had a sick spell and was in the hospital. And the hospital said, "You can't take her back to her house, because she can't function without outside help." So that was it. We told mother, "We're getting you out of the hospital and into better surroundings." "Oh, good, I'm going home." "No, you can't go home right now because you're not well enough. So we're taking you to Zenon, where they'll give you real good care. And we'll just see how that works out." That got her in.

In Zenon, she had every opportunity to use the telephone. And she used it a lot. She would call and say, "I'm ready to go home. Come and pick me up and take me home." "But I'm in Springfield, Mother . . . " At this time, she was also going through the transition of becoming a resident of the nursing home. She'd fight the nurses. She was a big, strong person and she had a lot of spirit. The nurses would treat her like a child from time to time. And that would make her unhappy. So she'd cry or punch 'em — one or the other. When she would tell me what she did, I would scold her and then she'd say she wouldn't do it anymore. And then she wouldn't be as physical as she had been the one or two times when she socked them. We were sometimes afraid that the nursing home wouldn't keep her, but the home never complained about her behavior. Mother was just one of many.

Even though mother was in the nursing home, she still had her house. And she'd ask about it all the time. "Are you still taking care of the house? Are you watching it?" (We were watching it. Well, we were having the farm operator watching it.) The house has been standing there empty, but partly furnished for six or seven years.

I took her back to the house one time. I guess it was a slightly hazardous thing to do, but I took her to see the house. When we got there, she walked in and looked around. Then she sat down at the organ and played a few chords on it. She was just like a little animal finding her own place again. Then I said, "Okay, mom, we've got to go now." "You mean I can't stay?" "No, no, it's not ready for you and you're not ready either, so let's go. We've gotta go now." And I hustled her out of there. We had dinner and then I took her back to the nursing home. She didn't resist going back, but she raised the roof over the telephone later. That sort of upset me, but I wasn't sorry that I took her back to the house. However, I don't say that it was a smart thing to do. It could have been a pretty nasty scene.

I don't think mother ever really accepted the nursing home. She really felt that she was being held against her will. So one day, she called the governor of the state, who happened to be her cousin. She got the governor's office all right, but she wasn't satisfied with the attention they gave her. So she made it very clear that the governor *was her cousin*! Well, they checked hurriedly and found that, in fact, she *was* the governor's cousin. Then they switched her to the governor's personal secretary, who took all kinds of information from her. Afterwards, the governor's office got in touch with the nursing home. And that caused a bit of commotion at the home. She sure had them shook up! You know, in a way, we were all kind of proud to realize that someone had taken her seriously.

When mother was first in the home, we would come out to visit her on a weekend. We'd take her out for dinner and then take her for a ride through the countryside. She just loved to drive around in the car. We'd stop at the cemetery and visit the graves. We'd see the home and find out how the farm was. She really cared more about the home in Monroe, though — the home she was born in. It was still standing, but abandoned. She would talk and talk and talk about it, because she was more lucid and capable then. And she would talk and talk and talk. But each time we went out, she had gotten a bit more frail. So we finally had to quit taking her out of the home.

Mother is really mellowed. She's not abusive at all now. She'll be 91 this coming month. She's in a wheelchair. And she doesn't talk much any more. Sometimes I'll play the harmonica for her when I go to visit. And when I get all done, she'll say, "You still have your dimple." That's a long sentence for her. Mother doesn't talk much because she isn't really up to date. She's not even watching television or trying to keep current. She's pretty dormant now. It's like her life has closed down. Mother's not really lucid any more and her voice has changed to a weak gutteral sound.

I don't know how many people she recognizes. First off, her vision is nowhere as good as it was. And the forgetfulness of age is really catching up with her. The next generation of Hannons is coming along now. The babies — great grandchildren — have all been brought out there for grandma to hold. She's always loved babies. So for her to hold Johnny — Ellen's son — was really fine. And I think she knew it was her great grandson. We have a picture of mother with Ellen, and mother's holding the baby. We're going to have a copy made for her. I think she will like it. Although I'm not sure she will pay much attention to it. She doesn't have a lot of personal things in her room. Everything is the thrill of the moment. There's nothing like actually holding that baby. I think that's really her attitude.

Mother didn't really like it when we would send her flowers. "Well, what good are flowers. I mean, they're just flowers." Flowers used to have a certain romantic appeal for her. My dad was good about flowers. He would bring her flowers for birthdays and anniversaries and so forth. And she liked that. But when he died, a lot of those little niceties went with him. She was bitter about the whole thing. She thought flowers were the substitute for a visit. Boy, she could call a spade a spade. So she said, "Don't bother sending me flowers if you're not coming. Just don't come out."

She was saying that sending her flowers wasn't going to make her feel any better and it wasn't taking her home. She wanted to go home or to have us visit her. I felt that if she didn't want flowers because they were a frustration to her, there was no sense in sending them. She was telling us "Don't bother with the flowers, but come out as often as you can," which is what we always did. If you think you're doing the right thing, you can't possibly feel guilty. Regret, remorse — whatever you want to call it — yes. But guilt, no.

Did I ever dread going back the first time after mother became a permanent resident of the nursing home. I didn't know what I was going to get hit with. That was where my wife, Mary, came in handy, having just gone down that road herself. The first time we were there — at this time now, mother was recovering — she was in good condition. She had no infirmaties. She was on her two feet and pretty feisty. And when we arrived — we had called ahead to tell them we were coming — she was very happy to see us. She said to whoever was with her, "I want you to meet my son," and so on. Every time it was this way. But then she'd raise hell about how badly they treated her. Tell us how they were and what cruel things they did. They'd hide her clothes — all these things. But, by golly, when we arrived, she had her best foot forward. She'd introduce us to her friends and to the nurses and they'd all make a big fuss. But the minute the nurses turned their backs, she'd talk about those "rotten kids." But in front of everyone, everything was hunky dory.

If mother had a bruise or something, we would ask about it. The only reason for asking about the bruise would be to try and find out if they threw her down the steps or something. If there was such a thing as cruelty in that nursing home, we weren't aware of it. We don't feel that there was ever any incidence of abuse. We also felt that *she* was going as far as *she dared*. And we would chew her out thoroughly. Mother was planning to escape most of the time. She talked about how she'd get out of that window. It was all first-floor stuff, you know, so we really didn't have to worry about it. She didn't need a ladder or anything. But she was always going to escape. Then the next time we came out, she'd say, "Lois always runs away. She gets in her wheelchair and she goes down the street there and they always have to go out and get her. She always runs away. She always tries to run away."

It's easier for me to go there now. It's just another place I have to go. She's so old, so frail, and there's so little that seems to be going on in her life. I feel more like I'm going because I should go. And yet I know that when I do go there, I'm going to try to entertain her by talking to her and just being there or by bringing her a little treat. Ice cream, or something like that. Or I can bring some pictures of Johnny. And that's fine. She has a thrill then. The only thing is, what happens the rest of the days that I don't come? I just have to feel that nature has a way of making things work. And, very likely, if you have meat and potatoes seven days a week for 40 weeks and then you get some ice cream, you'll say, "Oh, it tasted kind of good after all that meat and potatoes." I think that's how basic it is. I really don't think that I am important to her.

I don't feel sad until I'm leaving. I'm sort of sorry that this is such an unnatural way to live, because she's in such a protected environment, that nature has been practically stopped. Her body goes right on living — living beyond her mental use for her body. So she is being given an environment and a contact with the world for as long as she lives, which is fine. But she's getting very little out of it. That doesn't mean that I would want her put out of her life. It's just that we wonder what is the usefulness of it. And yet we can also say that she gets up in the morning and seems fine. And she's eating her meals. By golly, she likes to eat her meals. At 91 years old, eating ice cream or eating your breakfast is a pleasure. So she *is* getting her pleasure.

I'm an emotional person. But I don't feel super sad or depressed. At one time, music and such things were important to my mother. Then when my dad died, it abruptly stopped. I mean 99 and 44/100 percent of my mother's life died with my dad. And the other 56/100 percent remained, and what is left is really more animal-like now. Even to hold a baby is an instinctive reaction, which is the same as that of an animal — a female animal.

I wouldn't want to live the way my mother's living. I would rather die at 80 in my own house than live to 90 in a nursing home. Unfortunately we don't have this kind of control over our lives. So my feeling is that if I'm able to take care of myself at 75 or 80 and then need some suggestions from my kids, then I'd better take those suggestions. The ones they give me then are going to be more helpful to me at that age. If I go another four or five years beyond that, my kids won't be giving me suggestions, they'll simply be taking over. So it's best that I go with the suggestions now, than comply with orders later. We tried to offer things to my mother that would have made her life easier. But since nothing was going to work — as far as she was concerned — she lost control. We took over. We said, "That's it," and we just made the decisions for her.

I probably will live long enough that I'll end up in a nursing home. And I do think that this experience with my mother would probably be enough to help me during my time in the home. I'm more or less accepting of the situation. I think that if you feel a nursing home is where you are going to live out your last few years, you're going in with a better attitude.

When I get old enough that a nursing home is the best place for me, I think I'll probably make the best of it. I think I'll have a very good time while I'm there. I'll be fairly boisterous. I'm gonna take my harmonica and be the life of the party. I'll probably be a nuisance, for that matter, but I don't think I'll be belligerent. I'm just as crabby as my mother, but I think there's a difference between being crabby and crochety and being downright belligerent.

Now I always thought of my mother as an outgoing person. And I think she was. The only thing is, she also tended to be the authority. Now, I'm in an occupation where I'm a paid authority. But I think that being the "authority" is something you have to clear away before you hit the age where you're going to a nursing home or to any other place of communal living. You just have to submerge this particular characteristic — be it an asset or a fault. Some day you're going to have to give up authority, so it's nice if you can replace it with something else. Just giving it up — that's no fun. I'd replace it with just clowning around and, probably, with doing something that involved myself with myself, whether it's whittling or playing the harmonica or fishing. Satisfying myself and not worrying about the rest of the world.

Looking back, yes, I have some scars from the experience. I don't mean from the nursing home bit. I mean the scars caused by my mother's infirmity. I can't really take her as infirm as she is. It's strange the kinds of things that trigger pain.

Sometimes when there is a real good soprano in the church choir, I choke up. You see, mother sang at weddings and funerals and she always sang the Star Spangled Banner at local events. So when I hear a really good soprano, I feel that I am witnessing the prolonged, living death of a person who was once one thing and who now is nothing. And in witnessing her living death, I end up being a weekly mourner.

I sometimes resent that I can't go to church without crying.

IT WAS A LABOR OF LOVE

Martin Ewing and his sister, Nancy, made a pact that their elderly parents would stay in their own home as long as it was humanly possible. With the unexpected death of his sister, Martin — though in poor health himself — assumed total responsibility for his mother and father. Martin's story is about love, commitment, adversity, and a pact that was never broken.

My mother was a Queen. She really was. Mother was raised in a well-to-do family, went to private schools as a young girl, then studied voice in Europe. She also traveled throughout the world. Finally, she met and married my father, who came from an exceptional family himself. First came my sister, and then I arrived.

We had a wonderful childhood. My mother was talented and my father was quite successful in business. They also had many friends. I adored my mother and my grandmother — who lived with us — and my sister. And I loved my father very much. Sure, we had disagreements like any family does. But my father never raised his hand to me or my sister. My mother would sometimes give me a spanking, but that's what children get. My sister was revered by my grandmother. According to her, the sun couldn't come up without checking with my sister first. My sister and I had sibling rivalries and so forth, but we were like two peas in a pod. When we were children, if I got sick, it was four or five months, and then she'd get the same illness. If she got sick, I'd get it probably within three weeks. It was weird. Chicken pox, mumps, measles, appendicitis — you name it. This would happen to both my sister and myself. She was 18 months and two days older than I.

My father was 88 when he passed away. He had been horribly ill for almost four years. He got sick in 1975 and he passed away in 1979. My mother had also been ill. She was hurt in an accident in a downtown department store, when an escalator broke. She went headlong down the escalator steps. My sister — who was behind her — tried to grab her. Fortunately, though, my sister didn't get a hold of her because if she had, I think both of them would have been hurt very badly. I was away at the time. When I came home, I found my mother in the hospital. She looked like someone had beat her with a sledgehammer. In the hospital, one thing lead to another and, very shortly, my mother had her first stroke. She was 70 at the time. During the next 16 ½ years, mother had 19 strokes. The doctors attributed the strokes to the old escalator injury, which she never really recovered from. At the end, she was just like an infant. There was nothing you could do for her.

Part of my mother's expenses were paid by the insurance my father had on her. Finally the insurance was used to the limit and the rest had to come out of pocket. When my father became ill, part of his care was paid for by insurance. When it was finally used up, the rest, again, had to come out of pocket. Eventually, all the money was gone. It doesn't take long to eat up tons and tons of money — especially when you've got nurses around the clock. It got to the point that even the income from the business and from other sources was not enough. So, at a certain point, it was my money being used. Yes, it was expensive, but I don't regret it. Not at all.

Before they became ill, I would see my parents on the average of twice a week at least — sometimes more — depending on whether I was out of town, or whatever. After they became sick, I saw my mother and father every day. Often, I'd go up and see my sister, who lived in the same building. They lived in a large high rise in the center of the city. During the time my parents were ill, I had a regular routine. I knew that every day I would go to see my parents for whatever amount of time I could spend with them. If my schedule meant I could spend only 45 minutes there, all right. If it meant I could spend an hour and a quarter or an hour and a half, that's what I did. Sometimes I would go there at lunch time to have a sandwich with my dad. Or sometimes I would have a salad with him and then eat when I got home. I'd do it just so he would have someone to talk to. In that way, he would know that he wasn't all alone, as he was not permitted visitors nor could he conduct any business on the phone.

My mother had hardly any company. She was a beautiful and very, very vain woman, and she didn't want people to see her in the condition she was in. Well, a lot of her friends even stopped calling her, and I resented that. If they were such good friends, they certainly should have called. Oh, they would call me now and then or my sister. But I resented the fact that some of my mother's very, very close friends stopped even calling to see if they could come to visit her. I thought, "That's not friendship. That's a lot of lip service."

My sister and I made an agreement when my father took sick that we would never put either of them in a nursing home — regardless of what it took. Somehow, some way, we would manage to see that they stayed in their own home — as long as humanly possible. My sister and I shared the responsibility for our parents when they were both ill. Since she lived in the same building, she handled everything in the house — overseeing the nurses, seeing that the house was taken care of, and so forth.

When my father took sick, I also took over his business, handling it as well as my own business. I saw to it that whatever their financial needs were, they were met. Even though I never particularly liked his business, I took it over because my father had asked me to take care of his clients, as well as the people he had done business with, for 64 years.

Since I had made dad that promise, I'm still taking care of the business — to this minute. During all of this time, I have lost only three of his accounts. One died, one moved away, and I threw one out. If anything happens to me, the business will go to a young man who had been taught the business by my father. And it will be given to him, which will result in a nice, sizable income. That's the way my father wanted it. And that's the way it is going to be. I've already given the young man a contract to that effect. And every one of the clients knows about it.

My sister took sick in late February of 1978. She died on the 13th day of May. I was in the hospital, totally paralyzed, at the time. I didn't know how bad my sister was when I entered the hospital. Though I knew she was not going to live long, because she had cancer, I figured from 60 to 90 days, from the way the doctors were talking. And 11 days later, she was gone. It was a horrible shock to me. There had been no one to take care of my parents, except my sister and myself. And I was totally paralyzed.

I am very family conscious, yes I am. I saw very great love in my wife's family. I never saw that kind of love in any family before I got married. It was really beautiful. Just beautiful. I admired it and respected it. My wife is extremely close to her aunts — one in particular — and I think they feel the same way about me. I'm especially fond of a first cousin of my wife. In many ways, she has filled the terrible void left when my sister died. She acts and talks to me just like my sister did. I feel that God has blessed me with her.

When my father looked like he was going to die, when it really got touch and go, I said to my wife, "Get Neal here." My parents loved our kids so much, so she called my son and he came immediately. Harriett, my daughter, was at the point where she couldn't come home, she was graduating from medical school. So she just couldn't get away. But Neal came, and it was important to me to have him here. He's a good, strong, lovable young man.

I don't really know if mother was told that my sister had died. I don't think that my mother ever realized that my sister was gone. But my mother was in no condition to have any other heartache or worry or sadness. She kept saying, "I want to go home," meaning she wanted to go to St. Louis, then she would say, "I want to go up and see mother." Well my sister was the picture of her mother — my grandmother — and she lived eight floors up in the same building. When mother said that, I'd always say, "Well grandma isn't here," or "your mother isn't here." I just didn't want to upset her. If she didn't know, so be it.

After my sister died, I had a responsibility that nobody else could help me with. It was nobody's responsiblity but mine. I couldn't ask my wife to forgo her obligations and responsibilities at the university, and my children weren't here. Neither my wife nor my ex-brother-in-law were inclined to take care of my dad and mother, which was perfectly okay with me. I mean that's the way it was.

My wife had good reason — to a certain degree — why she wasn't doing anything. I didn't take any cognizance of it, other than to accept her reasoning as valid. It had to do with an unfortunate event that had occurred many years before. My wife was always courteous to my parents. She was always thoughtful. Barbara just felt, "All right, let them live their lives and I'll live mine." That was the end of it. There were no recriminations one way or another.

I was sad about the situation, because I personally didn't feel that either of them — my wife or my parents — were wrong. "Okay, if that's the way it'll be, that's the way it'll be. And that's the way it was. It was a terrible thing. It was just one of those things that should never have happened in the first place. After my father died, everyone said, "Why don't you put your mother in a nursing home." I would never have put my mother into a nursing home, even if it had taken every penny I had. Under no circumstances! I wanted her in her own surroundings where, if she was able to comprehend or did comprehend anything, she saw her own pictures, her own furniture — everything that was hers. I was happy to take care of my mother. It was a burden, though not a burden that was hard to swallow. I mean it was difficult because I had a business of my own to take care of and I had mother's house to run. I had my own home and I had my own family. And you can just go so far.

Five months after my father died, I moved my mother from the downtown apartment building in which she lived to the building in which my wife and I live, so that I could take better care of her. It wasn't that I wanted to get rid of her apartment downtown. It's just that it made it much more convenient and easier for me to handle. I knew that as time went on my mother was certainly going to get worse. She was never going to get better. And if something happened, I was three floors away from her. I wouldn't have to run downtown to get to her.

It was a tough move. I never realized there was so much junk in any house until I started packing it up and getting it moved. Ohhhh it was horrendous for me! Well I packed everything with the help of the nurses — her dishes, the lamps, her little art work, the pictures, you know, and her clothes and other things. Sure, the nurses helped me, but it wasn't just the way I wanted to do it. I knew how I would want it done in my own home and I wanted to do the same for my mother's stuff because she treasured a lot of it. So I did it. I had movers take most of the stuff and bring it here. But the fine things I put in my own car and brought them — the good crystal and so forth. My mother had given a great many of her things to my sister, before my sister passed away. That was her privilege. It was hers to give. And, so be it. She did some things that my father was very upset about — with her jewelry and so forth. I said to him, "Look it's hers, and nobody has a right to say she shouldn't have done what she did." So that was the way it wound up. And that's it.

It had been a very difficult five months after Dad died, because it meant every day I had to run downtown, not only to oversee the finances, but I also had to see to the nurses, to the food, and to whatever else was necessary. My mother had the same around-the-clock nurses here as she had had downtown. One of these nurses was with my mother 16 ½ years from day one, until the day she died. The second nurse had been with us for more than 10 years, and the third for over seven. I was very fortunate to have people I could really count on.

If anything came up — if I were out of town on business — the nurse on duty would call the other two, who would rush there immediately, day or night. They would call the doctor immediately, with absolutely no hesitation. The doctor who was taking care of her adored my mother. If he got called, as fast as he could get hold of his bag and his hat and coat, he was on his way to my mother's home. A number of times when I got emergency calls, he would already be there, waiting for me maybe 40 or 45 minutes. He would not leave without seeing me and discussing the situation with me.

Caring for my mother was a lot of work, a lot of burden, and a terrible anxiety for me. After my father died, I saw my mother every solitary day, unless I was out of town. I didn't care what time it was, I went there. I truthfully don't know whether she knew where she was or not, or even recognized me from time to time and, after I moved her, I just don't think she was capable of understanding she was in a different place. But her surroundings were hers. And that's what I wanted for her. Sometimes I could talk to my mother and her eyes would tell me whether she understood me, or at least recognized me. Other times it was like talking to a wall. A lot of times, mother would talk to me in whatever fashion she could. So often, it was garbled, so I would question her and watch her eyes. When her eyes lit up, I would know I was hitting the mark. I would do it that way to bring out what she wanted to communicate. When she would give me a little smile, I would know that's what she wanted to tell me.

There were many times that I left mother's apartment and felt like jumping out the window, because I wasn't sure she even knew I was there. I wasn't sure that she realized what was going on around her. But I needed to check to see what she needed. Did she need some new things — nightgowns or slippers or whatever? I just wanted to keep my mother in a proper way. I wanted her to look good. The nurses kept mother looking like a doll. Her hair was done twice a week and her fingernails were manicured, because that was the way my mother was. It made me feel good to see her that way. I played it by ear. As far as I was concerned, if she was not in pain or in any great difficulty other than she was an ill woman, so be it. So let her live her life the best it could be.

After each stroke, my mother seemed to get a little bit worse. And there came a time after my dad died that the doctor requested that I take guardianship of my mother. It was necessary so that I could authorize medical care for her legally. My wife also thought it was best, when we discussed it, because somebody had to be able to say, "Yes, do this," or "No, don't do that." I discussed it with my attorneys and they thought it was the proper thing to do.

I went to court to get guardianship. It was not an easy thing to do . Believe me. To do it, I had to declare my mother incompetent. I *did not want* to declare my mother incompetent. So I said she was competent, but that she was just incapable of doing things for herself — physically. Mentally, there was no way of determining whether she understood me, and just couldn't converse with me because of her strokes, or whether she didn't even understand me. Nobody was able to ascertain that, not even the doctors. From time to time, she would be able to talk for a few moments and make sense. Other times, she would just sit mute.

Now the court has what is known as a guardian ad litem, who is an officer of the court — an attorney — who is appointed by the judge to investigate the application for guardianship. The officer of the court goes and questions and checks the surroundings in which the person is living. The particular attorney that was appointed in this case happened to be a very lovely young woman who had lost her husband about a year before. She came over to mother's apartment. I was there when she walked in, and I pointed to my mother. I wasn't going to say anything one way or another. I was just going to let her find out what she wanted to know.

This young attorney went over to my mother's bed — an electric one I had gotten for her — and raised it to where she could sit next to mother and talk to her. She took my mother's hand and began talking to her. My mother was looking at the attorney, but I didn't know if she was understanding the young woman or not. But I will say this, sometimes a person's voice — tone or resonance — got through. Sometimes my voice got through, sometimes it didn't. You never knew if she would be able to talk or if she would talk. This young attorney started talking to her. And she said, "Are you being taken care of well?" My mother looked at her with a sort of contempt. And I thought, "Oh, boy!" Then the attorney said, "Do you love your son?" And as clear as a bell, my mother said, "You bet!" And I nearly fell out of the chair. Honestly, I started to cry, the nurse started to cry, everybody did. For four months, I hadn't heard my mother utter a word. It was incredible. The attorney asked my mother a number of other questions. Then she said, "Do you think your son loves you?" And my mother said, "Absolutely!" A word like that I hadn't heard my mother utter in at least two years — at least, maybe longer. It really threw me. The whole day was shot to hell.

I then had to go to court. It was the Chief Judge of the probate court who heard the case. I had already been warned that he was very, very strict and very tough on anyone getting guardianship. He was that way because of any monies or whatever might be involved. I was sitting there in court, and he called the attorney to the bench and asked her to report on what she found. He said he wanted to ask her a few questions on her written report. Then he motioned for me to come up in front of the bench. When I went up there, he said, "I want you to know that — in maybe three out of a hundred, maybe three out of a thousand cases — I allow something of this nature. I have yet to see a report come across the bench such as the one presented by the guardian ad litem. You are to be commended. I would only hope that there are people who do and act the way you have toward your parents — especially your mother who is still living. You are given guardianship with my blessing."

From time to time, I had to sign certain forms and provide certain information and documentation to the court. But nothing changed after I became guardian. I was not doing anything different than I was before. It was just a matter of doing it legally. Before this, I didn't have the right to do certain things or give orders for medical care. Nobody had questioned my actions, but my mother still had a brother who she hadn't spoken to in years — that nobody in the family had spoken to. But he was still her brother and had certain rights. I never wanted my uncle to have the opportunity of saying, "I don't want this" or "I don't want that," because if you would say something is white, he'd say it was black. If you agreed with him, you were wrong because you agreed with him. I mean, he never agreed with anyone in his entire life. I had no problems with the guardianship arrangement — once the decision was made. It was a beautiful experience for me.

I was out on the west coast when my mother passed away. My wife and I had gone out there to see our daughter and son-in-law. When my mother died, the nurse tried to reach me, and when she couldn't, she was able to reach my daughter. My daughter didn't know where to find us — my wife and I — because we were out of the hotel. But we were all going to meet later for a cup of coffee, and when I saw my daughter coming down the street to meet us, with her husband coming along behind her, I knew something was wrong. He was not expected to be with her. When she walked up to me, she said, "Dad, I

have some bad news." I just looked at her and said, "Oh my
God, no!" I knew what it was.

We rushed back to my daughter's apartment to get a hold of
the nurses. I called home and, of course, the nurses were crying their eyes out. Well, my mother had passed away. I say it
was a blessing. I don't think she was suffering, although I
really don't know. It was just a matter of how long she was going to be able to hold out. I figured that the length of time that
she was ill had been more than enough.

I was very torn up, though. I had not wanted to make that
trip. In fact, something told me not to go. But I have an obligation to my children, too. So I had gone. Of course, there's
nothing to say, that, had I been in town at the time, I would
have been at home. I don't feel guilty about not being here. I
just feel bad that it happened while I wasn't home. That's all.

It was very difficult breaking up mother's apartment — getting rid of things I knew she loved. In fact, I didn't start breaking up her apartment for a couple of months. I didn't have the
heart to go down there and start tearing the place apart. Going
down there didn't bother me. I just didn't know what I really
wanted to do with mother's things. The apartment was there. I
thought about how to do it, and then I would think, "No, I'm
not going to do it that way." I couldn't make up my mind what I
really wanted to do. It took me two months. Finally I made up
my mind and said, "Well, it's not doing me any good sitting
here. I might as well do it. Once it's over, it's over with. That's
all. It may give me a little peace of mind, too." That's the only
way I could think of it.

One of my cousins had said, "Well, why don't you sell this,
sell that, or give this to University Hospital and let 'em put it
in their thrift shop?" "I said, "No way, if I'm going to give it,
I'm going to give it. I'm not going to attach a monetary value
to it." There were certain things I wanted to give to certain
people, which my mother wanted me to do. Then I decided
what I wanted to do with other things that she had never men-

tioned. Giving to people or giving to charity. And that's why I
decided that certain personal things of mother's would go to
the nurses. They took care of my mother even more than me.
The nurses loved the things I gave them. They thought they
were beautiful. I hope they enjoy having them. I gave some of
the things to my son for his home and I gave some things to my
daughter. Because I know my mother wanted them to have the
things. She would have done it herself. I kept some things for
myself. It was sad to see my mother's things going in different
directions. And it was final as when I came home and buried
my mother.

A lot of our friends thought I was a little bit nuts to do what
I did. I could care less what they thought. It's what I thought
that was important. All I can say is that I know how I felt toward my parents and what I wanted to do. I was going to have
only one mother and father. And they had always been there
for me when I needed them. I had been terribly ill myself. I've
been paralyzed three times. People still say to me, "You spent a
fortune." Yes, so what? When I needed help, my parents were
always there. They never stinted on anything.

This is something I don't think many people would want to
go through. It wasn't easy, but at the same time, it was a labor
of love, because my parents were good to me and good to my
sister. We both loved them very much. I also respected my
parents. And I believe that most children — although I'm not a
child — would want to take care of and do for their parents.
Some people don't. So be it because that's their make-up and
character. I wasn't raised that way.

All I can say is that I did what I wanted to do. Other people
— and I'm sure they have reasons of their own — feel differently. I don't castigate them or chastise them for their way of
thinking. That's up to them. Each person has to live with himself. I have to live with myself. If anyone had come up to me
and said, "You shouldn't do what you're doing," I think my first
reaction would be to punch them right in the nose. What right

would they have to tell me what to do? That was what I wanted to do. It is what my sister wanted to do. What we agreed we wanted to do together, if we were both here.

There is some possibility that taking care of my mother and father affected my own health. My wife, some of the family members, and a couple of very, very dear friends felt that it ran me into the ground. As far as they were concerned, my taking care of my parents was like an obsession. It wasn't. My wife and I talked about this from time to time, because she thought it was running me down — wearing me down would be more like it. She thought it was a terrible obligation that I had assumed — that it was too much for me to handle. I said, "Well, that may be your opinion, but it's not mine." Taking care of my parents was something that I felt was my responsibility. Nobody else could do it, so I was going to do it — period. I didn't ask anyone's permission. I just decided that I was going to do it. I wasn't being forced to do it. I could have washed my hands of it any time. I could have said, "Well, I'll put them in a nursing home." No. I didn't want that. I did what I wanted to do because I thought it was best for my parents. And for no other reason.

But I want to say here, that I do resent people — whether they be relatives or friends — putting elderly people into a nursing home or in some other place for someone else to take care of them and then more or less dropping them, and deciding that the person is someone else's responsibility. I can't see that. The reason I feel as strongly as I do is that my sister and I made that verbal agreement that, if something happened to one of us, the other would take care of our parents — in their own place — as long as possible.

All I can say is that I presume there are times when people have no alternatives due to the fact that they can't do it financially. This is a possibility. But at the same time, I think to myself, "Well, what's to stop them from taking the person into their own homes and taking care of them?" Now I'm using as an example my mother-in-law, whom I loved dearly. She lived just a block-and-a-half from us. When my mother-in-law was alone, I said to my wife, "What the hell, your mother's alone, have her come and live with us. We'll get a larger place or whatever." My grandmother lived with us for many, many years and our house wouldn't have been the same without her. Barbara's mother could have come and gone as she wanted. If she wanted to have a boyfriend, let her have a boyfriend. It made no difference to me. But my mother-in-law said that two families couldn't live under one roof. Well, this I've heard many times before, and it may or may not be true. When my mother-in-law was ill, and when we knew she wasn't going to live, I said to my wife, "She can't stay in that apartment alone." But Barbara's mother said, "I'm not going to leave my apartment. I'm going to stay right here in my bed." It was important to her. After my mother-in-law died, I said to my wife, "I don't think we should ever have let her talk us out of coming to live with us."

I know my wife and children were concerned about me, but they never said, don't do this or don't do that. They may have talked about it amongst themselves, but at no time did they ever bring it up to me. Very frankly, if they had brought it up, I don't know what I would have said at the time. I don't know how I would have reacted. In retrospect, I probably would have said, "Look, you're not obligated to do it, so don't talk about it." I probably would have answered them in that manner.

My wife never mentioned that she thought it was taking time away from her. She's never mentioned that. If she felt that way, she had every reasons to say it. I don't believe I shorted my family — my personal family — in any way, shape, or form. I didn't take away financially from my family. I didn't take away my love. I didn't take away from the time I spent with them — as far as I can remember. Maybe I was a little less pleasant than usual at times, because I might have been tired or worried. But my family — my children and my wife — were always as important to me as they were before my parents go sick. And I never would have taken away from my wife for my mother. Nor would I have taken away from my mother because my wife wanted something unusual. They were both equal, as far as what I would do for either one.

I didn't take anything from my normal living pattern for the time I spent each day with my mother. I didn't take away from my wife or my children or our friends. It just took a little added effort, on my part, each day to do certain things. So instead of going to bed at, say, 10:00 P.M., I went to bed at 10:45, or whatever. Or I got up a little earlier in the morning, so I could handle everything in the time that I had allotted to myself for my normal daily living plus the time I would spend doing other things for my parents.

I don't think I would do anything different if I had it to do over. I might change some things along the way, because I'm smarter today about certain things that happened — but for no other reason. Maybe philosophically, I might have handled things differently. My thinking might have been a little different about why I did what I did at the time. But I wouldn't change things.

I may have, at one time or another, wondered whether they really would be better off if I had gone this way or that way, in the care that I was giving my mother and father. Whether I did right or wrong, I really don't know. I tried to do what I thought was the best for them. Whether I did or not, I can't be the judge of that. When my father got ill, the doctors wanted to do additional surgery and I said yes. Maybe I shouldn't have said yes, I don't know. Based on what I was told and on the opinions of people who counseled me, I thought I did the right thing. They could have been wrong, too, I don't know. And I never tried to find out whether I was right or wrong. I still feel in my heart that I did what I should have done.

To this day, I think of my parents — both of them. I think

of my sister and I'm saddened. It's strange, I was the one who was so terribly ill for such long periods of time before my sister ever got sick — or my father or my mother. And I'm the only one left. That bothers me sometimes. It does. But that's the way the guy upstairs wanted it.

MY FAMILY IS FALLING APART

When Marty Hagen's mother moved into the Hagen home after a stroke, the stay was to be a temporary one. But that's not how it turned out. In the months that followed, grandma — never an easy person to get along with — disrupted the household, drove away the Hagen's friends, and almost destroyed the family.

Daughter Marty, her husband John, and their two children Johnny and Nan talk here about the changes in their lives and in their relationships since grandma moved in to stay.

Marty: Mother, who is 74 now, worked all her life — from the time she was 16, when her mother sent her out to work. Mother was smart, and she wanted to go on to school, to college. But two years in high school — business high school — was all they would let her have. So she had to find security for herself. Mother found a job and she worked at it until she retired. It was a good job, one where she could buy stock and things like that. So she became very self-sufficient.

My mother was married twice. She and my father were divorced when I was five, but they remained friends throughout my growing up. Mother didn't remarry until I was 20, and I think she was married only six or seven years before her second husband died. Roy was a wonderful stepfather. Mother has lived alone since my stepfather died, which is about 14 years now, I guess. She has her own house. The house is hers until she dies and then it goes to Roy's daughter from an earlier marriage — his granddaughter, really, because his daughter died very recently. Roy's will is very tight. The house is hers.

To my mother, money is a way of expressing love. When I was in the hospital and had surgery, and when my youngest nearly died, my mother never came to visit me. She wouldn't come to see me, but she would offer us money. She'd come over and say something like, "Could you use $10,000? Would you use it to finish the bathroom?" That's what she said last year, because we were building an upstairs on our house. Well, as soon as I take the money, I get the worst guilty conscience. I want to get rid of it as soon as possible, because it always comes back to me. "I gave you . . . ."

The money's not given for love. If we asked for it, it would be different. But we don't ask for it. She gives it to us and then she's got us. That's it. There's just no way out. If we didn't get that bathroom, it wouldn't have made any real difference. I mean, we have two other bathrooms in the house. I think this is all harder on John, even, than on me, because he works so hard.

Mother has always been very active. And when she retired, she didn't have a hard time making the transition from going to work to being at home. Her house was always so clean and neat. She belonged to the Senior Golden Age Group and she took senior citizen trips. She also cooked meals and cleaned house for a 90-year-old woman down the block. Mother would get very, very nervous if she didn't have anything to do. She couldn't stand it. She didn't watch television. "Television is a waste of time, except for the news, which is a repeat." Oh, she had a few things that she watched, like the movies — the eight o'clock movies. She didn't read, never enjoyed reading.

Last fall, my mother had a stroke, and she was in the hospital for some time. When she left the hospital, she didn't have control of her bladder. Regardless, the hospital wanted us to take my mother home. So we went down to the hospital's social service department, and I told them we couldn't take her home. That it was impossible. I asked if they could recommend a place where we could take my mother. The social worker said she couldn't make a recommendation, but suggested that we look at nursing homes and places like that. So we did. We shopped around for a nursing home, and we finally found one.

Mother was in the home from November until January, when Medicare payments stopped. And when Medicare stops making payments, the insurance company does too. When I got the bill for the last two months at the nursing home, it was $9,000. There's no way that we could have kept my mother in that nursing center. There isn't that much ready cash. There's cash, but there's not that much ready cash. The existing amount would last two-and-one-half months — tops. Then there's nothing.

When mother left the nursing home, she was more or less confined. She couldn't live in her own home by herself. So she moved in with us — on a temporary basis, we thought. But since she's been here, Mother has decided she doesn't want to live in her house any more. She wants this to be her home.

John: We know where our responsibility lies, as far as Marty's mother is concerned. She's a good woman. And the only real problem with her being here is that this is a pretty open house. A lot of kids are in here all of the time. Kids are coming and going. This is a noisy place. It's a fun house — at least it used to be.

There's something going on with the family all of the time. My children and my wife are ice skaters. Nan and Marty are both professionals, and they teach up in Westchester. Sally is a competitive skater, and our son, John, is too. John was at the Olympic Training School for almost a year-and-a-half. But last summer, he had a serious accident out there in Colorado. Before his accident, we thought that he would go on to the nationals this year and be, at least, a national champion. But because of his accident, he didn't make it.

Grandma's influence has been very strong in this house. And from the day she came, things were going to be run her way. She doesn't like to be disturbed. She doesn't like a lot of noise. After she came here, she didn't want anything going on around her. And yet that's really kind of false, too, because she likes people fussing over her. When the focus of attention is on her, then the parties are fine. When it's not, she complains. And she complains a lot!

Marty: We've had only two parties since mother came. One of them was Nan's 21st birthday party last week. We had friends here that Nan hadn't seen for years — ones she graduated from high school with. Not only does mother not want us to have parties, she also doesn't want me — or us — to do anything she can't do. If she can't go out to lunch, we can't. Two weeks ago was the first time since January that we were all out as a family. And that was because my aunt came over and sat

with mother. It was the first time we had been out, because mother doesn't want to let anybody out of her
sight.

Mother does little things to punish me. She had been
here about two weeks, when a friend called and said,
"Oh, come on, let's go out for dinner. Where do you
want to go?" Well, before we could leave for dinner, I
had to get my mom all ready for bed. Mother's paralyzed on her right side and it was a hassle.

Pat and I went to a paint store and looked at walltex,
because that's what I wanted to do. We also looked at
carpeting. Then we had a steak sandwich and talked,
really talked. We had two drinks. And talked and
talked and talked. I got home just in time for John to
go to work on the midnight shift. He had gone on
midnights when my mother came here, so I could go
back to work. Well, I walked in and found that mother
had wet the bed. And that's the punishment I get, if I
go out or if I'm a few minutes late coming home from
work. She threatens that she'll pee in the bed, and
then she does it.

Mother is trying to get rid of all my friends. Now, she
hasn't been as rude to anyone as she has been to Pat.
But she knows Pat cares — that she'll call. When Pat
calls or comes over, my mother feels that Pat is taking
me away from her. If my mother is sitting in front of
the television and I want to talk with Pat, or any other
friend, for that matter, we'll go into the back room. I
mean, you do need privacy. And this is where mother
gets rude. She wants me right there. If she gets rid of
all my friends, then what will I have? No friends. My

mother will say to my friends, "I don't like you because you drink too much." "We don't want you here."
"You're too cheap." She doesn't want to share me. Pat's
just about the only friend I have left. Nobody else
bothers much any more.

John: My brother won't come over either. I borrowed his
electric saw a couple of weeks ago to do some work on
the house. When I finished with it, he said, "Well, I
guess it's your saw now." I said, "What do you mean?"
He said, "Well, I'm not coming back while that old
bag is here." A little rough, maybe. But he won't come
through that door, and neither will my older sister.
They won't come here at all now because grandma's
here permanently.

If sombody comes over, and she knows some little
thing about them, she'll grill 'em. Well, they don't like
that. And a few people have told her, over the years,
"It's none of your goddam business." Grandma puts
the inquisition on my sister, Ann. For one thing, Ann
has six children, and grandma's told her that that's
despicable. "How in the world can you have six children? Are you some kind of sicko?" And Ann says, "I
love my children and it isn't any of your goddamed
business. I won't subject myself to listening to your
conversation." Grandma's been this way all her life,
but now its actually heightened, because she has
nothing else to dwell on.

Marty: I feel sorry for how mother is, but she did it herself.
Mother is the type of person who will ask 25 people for
their opinions, but then do what she wants to do. She
had had high blood pressure for years. She'd ask the

pharmacist and everyone else about the medicine she was taking. Then she decided to cut down on her medicine and started taking it every other day instead of every day. Then, maybe, it was twice a week. And then she decided not to take it at all.

John: Grandma thought the natural way was the best way. And, in some respects, it's true. But here's a lady who had high blood pressure — extremely high blood pressure. She's being treated by a physician and he's given her a prescription that she was absolutely supposed to take. And yet, she wouldn't do it. She said that the medicine made her feel crazy, or changed her mood, or whatever. It may very well have. Some prescriptions do this to you. But taking her medicine was something she should have done. A physical therapist who was treating grandma said to her in front of us, "You did this to yourself. If you had followed your medication instructions, you would never have had the stroke." Whether the therapist was right or wrong, I can't really say. If it wasn't the absolute cause of the stroke, I believe it was a contributing factor, at least.

When grandma first came home after the stroke, we made a big mistake by catering to her. We were too damn good to her. If we had let her sit for a while and stew in her own brew, and let her realize that there wasn't going to be someone running to aid her every second, we'd have been better off. Our mistake, first of all, was not to give her enough responsibility for herself. We helped her too much.

She had always been a real active, hardworking woman. Since I've mentioned a lot of her shortcomings, I should mention some of her better points. She's responsible and she's diligent. She's a product of her time, too. She grew up in the depression era, where the work motive was everything. If anyone sat down for any reason, he was lazy and shiftless. Sitting here right now would be a total waste of time, as far as she is concerned. Now, we are all readers in this family, but sitting down and reading a book is out of the question.

Grandma says she can't read. She can't read a magazine. It's too hard to read. But she gets the stock exchange page from the newspaper and right away she starts reading it. I can't even see it. She also loves those junkie tabloids. She reads them like they're the bible. All those goofy medical things. She used to bring them over before she was sick, and say, "Look at this, look at this." She loves those. And she loves that morning talk show host who talks about trashy sex and exploitation stuff. He's the only Irishman she likes, other than me.

It's pretty hard for people who have been married as many years as we have to reverse our lifestyle. Our lifestyle is just not the same as hers. It's very difficult. We don't want her to change her life. We're not trying to make her change. But god knows, living with her is going to be twice as tough because of her condition. She's got her pettiness, but then we all do. I sometimes like grandma. I sometimes don't. I never wished her dead, although there have been times when the thought crossed my mind.

Marty: John went on midnights to help me out, so I could go

back to work. Now the first two weeks, it was beautiful. I could say, "No problem." But that was only because mother thought I was quiting my job. The first day I went back to work, I stopped at the store on the way home to pick something up. When I got home, she had just wet the bed. She had done it because I wasn't home on time. It was just to keep me busy.

Another time, we were painting — John and Johnny were doing it. I was taking the girls to the doctor that morning and then I had a class to teach, which meant I was gone from 9:00 A.M. to about 2:30 P.M. Before I left, I put a diaper on my mother, because John and Johnny couldn't be upstairs painting and varnishing and then run downstairs every time whe wanted something.

I called John while we were gone, and he said, "Marty, we have almost been in a physical fight with your mother. She won't let us take off the diaper. When I got home — and as soon as we walked in — Mother said, "I peed five times." And I said, "Mom, you're not hurting me, you're hurting yourself. I'll take the diaper off right now and wash it, because you're going to get sore." "No!" She wouldn't let me do it. But when it's 5:30 and I'm making dinner, Sally comes in and says, "Grandma just peed all over your chair. So I figured she did get me. She's not hurting herself, because she knows when the diaper comes off — whenever that is — she's going to get washed again.

The night before, I had gotten so mad at my mother, I took Sally and Nan out for dinner. It was the first time the three of us had been out in a long, long time. We left at 6:30 and we got back at ten after eight. That will tell you that we had dinner and we came right home. As soon as I came in, mother was telling me to do this and to do that. She kept telling me what to do. And she also told me how many times she had peed.

John: Being hard to get along with really isn't because of her illness. Marty's mother has always been hard to get along with. She's never been real easy. She comes in and she takes over. She tells the kids what to do. Many times, I've said, "Wait a minute, mom, these are my children. They do it my way. They have their own ways of doing things. And if I don't find fault with them, you certainly shouldn't."

Marty: In the middle of getting her undressed that same night, mother shoved her upper plate at me. I didn't scream and I didn't yell, because that isn't going to do anyone any good. I just went into the kitchen, I kicked my foot up and my shoe flew across the room and broke the beautiful clock John had given me for our anniversay — an oak clock. I stood there watching it go crashing down. And I said, "Oh, my clock!"

Just then, Sally came running in. "I didn't touch her. I didn't have anything to do with it." I thought, "God, I didn't hear any noise." I went into the living room and found that my mother had gotten off the chair she was sitting on, walked across the room, sat down on another chair, and got it wet. But she did it. She can do things. Like I found she can take off her shoes and socks and her brace. She is also learning to dress her- self. She learned how to wash herself, but she won't do it. She won't wash her face and her hands, because they'll not be clean enough. I have to do it.

Nan: Having grandma here puts a lot of pressure on us kids as well as mother and dad. We can't come and go as we always have. We always have to be here. Someone has to be here. It's real hard on everybody. She likes to corner me and tell me how she feels about everybody.

Marty: My mother, she has always said to Nan, "If it wasn't for me, your mother and father wouldn't be married, because I went to see your grandmother and grandfather." Well, nobody made us get married.

Nan: I love my grandma, and I hate to say to put her in a home, but I think she should be kept away. Oh, not kept away, but I think she should try to live in her own house. Or else we should get someone in here to help us out.

I'm of age, and my parents give me full freedom to do whatever I want. And I've never done anything wrong in that they should take anything away from me. I could come in at six in the morning and they wouldn't care. But grandma waits up for me at night, because now I'm the only person that sleeps down here. She checks on me. She won't sleep until I'm here.

She just sits there and makes you feel guilty that you're going out or having fun. She doesn't think it's right. She tells my friends they drink too much if they have one beer. She tells me to stay away from boys. "Don't ever get intimate." "Don't do this, don't do that."

John: And grandma was a swinger.

Marty: Yes, I took more than one trip with my mother and her boyfriends.

John has always had a part-time job. We have committed ourselves to certain things. And he's always worked hard. His part-time job was one where he'd work from six to midnight two days a week. When you work days — as John did — that's an easy job, especially if you're a night person, which John is. But when you're working midnights, you're working your part-time job first and then your real job. Now John's a policeman and that's not the type of job you go to exhausted. He never stayed home. The days he worked his second job, John would say, "I have to work my part-time job, so I need to sleep." Well, I thought he was getting his sleep. But he wasn't. My mother would make him sleep on the couch and she would be in her room or in the wheelchair. When he'd just get to sleep, she'd want the TV guide, or something else.

One day, John was exhaused. He was getting sick. That was the time that his part-time job and his real job were going back-to-back. It was go to his part-time job, go to his real job, come home; go to his part-time job, go to his real job, come home. So that day, John just couldn't go to his part-time job. And he got canned. That was it. He had missed only two times in two-and-one-half years. Losing that job counted for a lot of money.

When mother's here, there is no way I can keep up the pace I used to. There is no way I can take care of her and do what I did before. So I lost a student, which was also a big chunk of money. Right now, we're down quite a bit of money. If John said to me, "You can't have your mother in the house," my mother would go. She wouldn't be her five minutes, if John said, "No!"

Mother is in a rehab center right now. When we took her there on Tuesday for some intensive therapy. I though, "Oh, my god, I'll be able to relax and get some sleep. Before she went, John and I couldn't sit and relax and talk in the evening. She wants to be with us. And by the time we get her ready for bed, we're both tired, and you figure you've ruined another night.

John: If we want to have a private conversation — just Marty and I — she'll say, "Secrets???????"

Marty: And does she have good ears! If John says, "Come on Marty, let's go upstairs," mother'll say, "Are you going to have a little nookie?" Forget it. Forget about having any sex life with your husband. For a while before she went to the rehab center, she insisted that I sleep downstairs. And I wasn't sleeping, because she kept ringing her bell.

John: Let me tell you about the bell. That was my mistake. When Marty and I first brought grandma home, her ability to communicate was very limited. She couldn't talk very well at all. If you had a conversation with her, you would have to sit down and sit there for a long time. And you would really have to work out what she was saying, which was okay. But just for con-

venience sake, I got her a bell. I gave her a little bell to
ring for assistance — if she wanted anything at all.
And she began ringing that bell like it was cowbell.

There was nothing wrong with her voice. She could
yell out if there was something wrong with her. As a
matter of fact, she just about blew me out of the room
a few times. If I twisted or something when I was trying to move her around, she would yell plenty loud.
So the bell became a weapon. If she had a thought on
her mind, she would ring that damn bell.

Finally, I said, "I'm going to get rid of that damn bell.
You don't need it." And boy! She went through the
roof! "Not only do I want the bell, I want a whistle,"
she said. And I said, "Over my dead body are you going to get a whistle." And she's never even going to see
another bell. One day, Nan's boyfriend took the
dinger out of the bell. And grandma blamed it on
Sally, our youngest daughter.

Apparently grandma reads the kids' personalities very
well. Nan is serious. She has very tender feelings. Sally's close to being a free spirit — not quite, but close.
She does what's in her mind. She does whatever the
hell she feels like doing. Her room is a disaster at all
times. I'll tell her to go up and clean it, and she'll say,
"As soon as I'm through with this." If I told Nan to do
it — even though she's 21 years old — bing, she'd be
in there doing it. Sally will be 14.

Sally used to have the best rapport with grandma. She
used to sit with her for hours. But one day, grandma
got short with her and started yelling and Sally said,

"I'm not going to take that. I don't have to. I'm not going to sit here and be browbeaten.

Marty: One time, Nan was doing the dishes, and grandma wanted Sally to dry them. Now I don't dry my dishes. I stack them on the sink and they dry just fine. But mother kept yelling at Sally and kept yelling at her. So Sally said, "You want me to do something grandma?" Then she turned on the radio and danced for her. My mother took her good foot and tried to kick Sally. You know, Sally doesn't care. She really doesn't.

John: Our son Johnny physically resembles Marty's father — a lot! He's a lot more placid in his disposition, but when Johnny gets a little riled, I can see quite a bit of grandpa in him. When grandma starts on Johnny, he just turns about and gives her the evil eye. And I know she's seeing grandpa. Then, if she wets her pants, it isn't on purpose. Grandma always backs off with Johnny. She does more backing off with him than she does with anybody else.

One day, I said to grandma, "Why are you doing this to our family? Because you're so miserable and sad, do you want everyone else to be miserable and sad?" She cried at that. And then I felt miserable. I mean I felt terrible that I made her feel that bad. But, on the other hand, I didn't feel that I said anything to her that she didn't have coming.

Johnny: I love my grandma and all, and she's always treated us kids well through the years, but when she came into this house, it was like a complete about face. I can see our family falling apart piece by piece. It's been like a vacation — a vacation at home — since grandma's been at the rehab center.

Marty: Mother's been gone since Tuesday, and we're still not relaxed. I'm still getting up at night. And I'm still nervous.

And, after 22 years, I feel that I'm watching my family being destroyed. I talked to the kids' doctor one day. And he said to me, "You know, I've watched your kids grow up. They're good kids. They have never given you any trouble. But you're going to lose your children. And John could divorce you. And you could have a nervous breakdown. Then, you're not going to have your children. You're not going to have your husband. And you're going to have a nervous breakdown. But you're still going to have your mother. Why are you doing this to yourself?" "She's my mother, and I'm an only child." "That's a guilt complex, and you shouldn't have it." He told me that, if I continue this way, I'm not going to have anything.

And that's the truth. The kids are escaping this. Instead of having their friends over now, they're going out because of the tension in this house. My kids aren't wild, but the house isn't the same anymore. I always liked my house. I don't like it anymore. I'm just trapped in it. All I can do is go to work, go to the grocery store, come home. My mother will change our lifestyle. She already has. I'll be thinking about something my mother has said or done, and when Nan says something to me, I'll snap at her. And Nan is the one that will cry if you look cross-eyed at her. The whole thing is that my mother is going to ruin our relationship. Ours is going to end up like my mother's and mine. I told my aunt once that I hated my mother.

John: When Marty's mother comes home, she'll be better than she has been in the past. I'm convinced she will be. I was talking to grandma just the other day. And in just those two days, I could hear the improvement. This rehab center is so highly touted by her therapists that I'm pretty much convinced that it's gonna work for her.

I think, if anything at all, she will be able to cope with this and be more comfortable with herself. I think that if she could just accept the fact that nobody is ever going to make any demands of her and she can just live her life out, she'll be okay. If she didn't have to compete all the time, she'd be a lot better off. Underlying, she's a good woman. She just doesn't have a very pleasing personality.

We'll have to get her in one of these day care centers, because she has to have some outside interests — not only for Marty's mental health, but also for hers. It's not because we don't want her here, it's because it's a physical impossibility to be able to provide her with all kinds of things to do. How many things can a woman who is partially paralyzed do? But if she has some organized outside interest — with people who know exactly what they can provide for her — I think it would be a damned good thing. It will be good for her and it will be good for Marty.

Marty: But if she doesn't want to go . . . .

John: She'll go, Marty. She'll go.

Marty: I looked into the day care center at Cottage and Temple Streets. But my mother says she doesn't like it, even though she went there for lunch once a week for years. I said, "Mother, if it was good enough to go there for lunch, why isn't it good enough for you to be there for the day?" But she doesn't want to go.

John: I don't think I'm going to give grandma any options. I'm not going to take crap from her. She's going to have to do things on her own.

Marty: They say mother can do it. The people at the rehab center feel that when mother comes back she will be able to wash and dress herself, transfer herself, and walk. I know she can walk by herself now.

John: I think it would be enough if she could just take care of herself and be able to do some things on her own. If she could just get out — just get away from the house for a while. I don't mean overnight. I just mean during the day. Go out with some group or whatever. Something to motivate her a little bit. This was all such an incredible shock to her. She went from being absolutely and completely independent — and very strong in that independence — to being totally dependent on other people. She's getting better, but it's such a slow process, and she's so incredibly impatient.

Marty: One morning when I was talking to John, I said, "You know, all I want is to have one morning that I don't have to get mother washed and dressed and fed before

I have my coffee. When mother was in the nursing home, she would never get dressed — ever. At home, the first thing she has to do in the morning is get dressed. On Saturday morning, I have to get up at 5:30 in order to be at work at quarter after eight. But lately, if I change my schedule in any way, she doesn't want to get up. She wants to wait. Last week, she said, "I'll wait for John to get home." Well, Johnny's home, but she just doesn't want to get out of bed. That morning, I'm ready to walk out the door, and all of a sudden, she wants to get up . . . NOW! and so I can't leave the house.

I would have to quit my job if John weren't working nights.

John: Even if the financial situation was such that my wife did not have to work, she would want to work. She takes a lot of pride in what she does. She enjoys it very much. It's very rewarding to her. It was something she took up not because she needed to at the time, but because she was a competitive skater when she was young and she enjoyed it.

Sometime ago, Marty said she was kind of bored and wanted some outside activity. While Marty doesn't profess to be a women's libber, I've always considered her my other half. We're equal. What she wants to do, she does. So I said, "Look around for something to do. Do something that will give you a little reward." So that's how she started teaching, and she's been at it ever since. She's taught national competitors. She's one of the highest rated, most well thought of pros in the Midwest. She's really very good and very, very well thought of.

As Marty said, I'm working midnights now because of this situation. And I'm not adapting too well. It's pretty hard for a guy who's been working days for the last 15 years to swing over to nights. It's kind of tough. But that's neither here nor there, because that's what has to be done now.

I want to teach our children that it's the right thing to take care of your parents, but not to the point of guilt. I don't want my children ever to feel it's a guilt thing. If I were in grandma's position, they would want to take care of me, but I would not want to be a burden to them. They're going to see grandma and think that all old people are like that.

My maternal grandparents lived in my parent's house until the day they died. Both of them. My grandfather was retired from the telephone company during the depression. He was the youngest retiree at that time. My grandfather had escaped from Ireland and he came over here. He had been an English teacher in the old country, but when he came here he wanted to be a teamster. So he drove a team of horses for the 'phone company. Then he retired and when he retired, he really retired. Oh, he did a few odd jobs, but he really enjoyed his leisure. He lived with my mother and father and they were great friends. Grandpa was my father's father-in-law, yet they were as tight as father and son. My father's father had died when he was a little boy, so he became close to my grandfather. They had a great relationship.

I remember my grandfather to this day. I would go into his room and we would sit there and listen to the

ball game together. I can also remember as a child going to visit him at the old railroad crossing, because
they always had a man who worked the gates at the
crossings. And we'd sit and talk for hours. I experienced my grandfather in a remarkable and good
way.

My grandfather was a great guy. And he loved parties. My mother and father would have parties in the
basement and grandfather would sit in a chair and all
the young people would come up and talk to him. And
he'd have a beer with them. The kids would always be
around him. He loved kids.

Grandma was a great baker. I'd come from school and
smell the bread baking. I'd come into that house and it
was great. Our house wasn't particularly big, yet we
crowded in somehow. And we all got along.

I do think that things could be the same way in our
house. I really do. But I think because of grandma's
personality it couldn't be exactly the same way. But I
can't see why she couldn't fit in in a harmonious way
with our mode of living. I think our mode of living is
very similar to that of my parents and their parents. I
know, that's a little pie in the sky.

Even if Marty's mother comes back from the rehab
center and she's at her best, she's still going to be difficult. We've known this for years, and we've accepted
it. That's the way she is. We knew this was going to be
a difficult situation when we brought her in. But nobody can understand how difficult it is until they've
lived with it. People have told me that, and now I un-

derstand it. I knew it was going to be difficult, but I
certainly didn't have any idea that it was going to be
as hard as it is. Hopefully, it will get better. I don't
doubt that she's going to be here forever. I'm pretty
sure she is.

I feel we're very responsible people and we would not
let grandma be put upon in any way, shape, or form.
She's been very good to us. She's my wife's mother,
and I felt like we had no choice but to take her in. I believe in the old oriental philosophy — you honor the
elderly. You respect their age and their years of learning. Experience is the world's greatest teacher. And I
feel you should honor your parents. I feel that to this
very minute.

I'll accept grandma back with no qualifications. I'm
willing to put up with all her difficult traits — and
they are extreme, believe me! But I'm going to do it.
No question about it. I'm going to accept it until the
day she dies. But I swear, she'll bury me. She's going
to be standing over my grave, tamping the dirt on top
of me.

Of course, we've considered a nursing home. But
we've never put it to her. I told her many years ago
that she'd always have a place. We always talked about
this being an inevitable thing. I knew that some day
she was going to be my responsibility. I knew this 20
years ago. I knew that some day I was going to have to
take care of her because Marty's an only child.
Grandma has nobody else.

I don't know whether we could afford it monetarily to

put grandma in a nursing home. It would be a real hardship. We had to supplement the cost of her being in the nursing home after her stroke. But if it got to the point where we couldn't possibly live with her — sure, we'd have to do it. It's not a moral thing with me. I'm not objecting to a nursing home on moral grounds. Nursing homes aren't like the old slave quarters or anything.

Did you ever see a movie called "Where's Papa?" You remember the feeling he had about his mother? He really wanted to kill her at times, but he couldn't ever bring himself even to say the words, "nursing home." I think there's a strong parallel here. I think that movie explains it as well as anything.

Marty: John has stronger family feelings than I have. He came from a large family. I lived with my grandmother and my aunt. I had two aunts and uncles — who, at one point, lived upstairs from us — so I always had a "father" in the house. I'm close to my aunts and uncles and my cousins. But they are still not brothers or sisters. I think John has closer feelings toward my mother than I do.

I don't know if anyone thinks that this kind of thing is really going to happen to them. One of my aunts said, "Keep your mother in the nursing home. You have to. Once you bring her to your home, you're not going to have a life." She hit it right on the nail. She said, "You don't know how hard it will be. Your mother never took care of anyone except herself." I remember, now, when my grandmother was sick, my one aunt took care of her for three months, my other aunt took care of her for three months, but my mother never took care of her. Maybe she would take her for a Saturday or a Sunday, but never more than that.

You're never quite prepared for something like this to happen to you. Everybody keeps saying, "This isn't going to happen to me." But it happens. Everyone is blind. Everyone is absolutely blind to this kind of situation. We ignore it. You know, we think, "If the time ever comes, we'll deal with it then." Then it's too late. John, you said for 20 years that you knew mother was going to come and live with us. Why didn't you get out the books and study? You said you knew it. I said, "No, it's not going to happen." We never prepared ourselves.

We didn't know anything about any family services that might exist. We didn't know to ask for information because we didn't know that it was available. We didn't even know that there were such things as rehab centers like the one mother's in now. We didn't know until the therapist came to the home and told us. And it was the therapist that told us we would have no problem with Medicare and with her other hospitalization picking up the tab. We didn't even know that.

The time demand with my mother — taking care of her — is no different than raising three kids. But when you raise three children, at least they don't tell you what to do. They don't yell at you. They don't belittle you. That's the difference.

John: You were younger then, too, and more capable of coping with it.

Marty: John, your Mother had a change of life baby and she
was very used to doing what she wanted to do by that
time. But when Jenny came along, she coped. You get
inner strength. You always have the inner strength to
dress somebody or change somebody. But you can't
take the mental pressure. That's the hard part. When
the kids were small, you just put them to bed when it
was time for them to go to bed. With my mother, you
can't put her to bed. She wants to be with us. You can't
sit and relax, and you can't talk.

John's my life. My house is not my life. My kids are
not my life, because they're getting older. They're
gonna have their own lives. John can retire in five-
and-one-half years. I don't want John to go on and
work after that until he's sixty-five and then drop over
dead the following week.

I'd like to go some place and just be with John. What
is marriage all about? You get married, you have kids,
you raise your kids and try to give them good morals.
But is that it? I want a life with my husband. He's not
worrying about all of this, but I am. I don't think my
mothers gonna die. I'm talking about, say, ten years.
And then what? That's really scaring me. It's not both-
ering him, but it's really scaring me!

(*Eight months later, Marty continues her story.*)

Mother came back from the rehab center being able to
do a lot more for herself. She can get herself dressed
and undressed, and she washes herself in the morning. She can also walk with a cane, but she still wants
the wheelchair in the livingroom. She can use the

phone. She does call people up, and she's able to talk.

Even though she can do more things, mother's still lonely. But she will not go to a day care center at all. John and I did bring her to the one right by our house. It's for day care only — like from 8:00 A.M. to 5:00 P.M. — and they have pick up and delivery service. When we went for an interview, mother insisted on having her wheelchair. She doesn't need a wheelchair now. When we got there, they wanted to see her walk. She told them she couldn't walk. It took three tries of falling back into the wheelchair before she got up. Then the staff asked her if she could feed herself, and she said, "No." I told them that the she couldn't cook, but she could feed herself. Next the staff wanted to know what medication she was on. She didn't know.

Beforehand, I had told the people at the day care center that mother didn't want to go anyplace. But the center told us that, without any effort on her part, they couldn't take her. It was a day care center, not an intermediate care center where they have the time to help people. It was a social place. The center had the attitude that, if mother didn't want to go there, they didn't want her. And the whole thing was, she just didn't want to go. So they said they "were sorry."

As for our family life. Now at least, we are coming and going as we want. There's no reason that we always have to be home with mother. She could go to a day care center, but she won't. Anyway, someone's usually home. But at least it's to the point that, if we want to go out, we just go out. And we did go on a vacation this summer. Nan stayed at home the first two weeks with my mother. And then I had somebody in for two weeks, so Nan could join us. When we got back, we found out that mother had given my cousin and his wife her house to live in. There had been a family reunion, and mother found out that my cousin was looking for an apartment, so she said they could move into her house. That house was my last hope. I had always hoped that, if things got too bad, she had a house, which was paid off, that she could live in.

A couple of weeks ago, I quit my job. Oh, I'm still teaching private students, but I'm not teaching classes any more. I just couldn't handle the pressure of ice shows and meetings and competitions. Before we went on vacation, I thought I was going to have a nervous breakdown. I'd love to be teaching classes, but I just couldn't get everything done. And with classes, you have to commit yourself for a whole year. I have a little more time now. I used to have classes on Sunday, but I don't have any now. And it's nice. It's been years since I've had a Sunday off. I don't get up at 5:30 or 6:00 A.M. any more, either. I wake up at 8:30 A.M. and have a cup of coffee before I get mother up. Now, mother is on my schedule.

John is back on days now, and he's working only one job. But whenever he can pick up an extra job, like the one he had this weekend, he does. On Saturday, when John had his side job, I went out and bought a book and went upstairs and I read all day. And the kids were upstairs with me. We're all just staying away from the situation — staying away from it in our own house. It's like being trapped. We've always eaten together, but Saturday we didn't. Since John wasn't home, I told the kids, "I'm going to fix something for mother, but I'm not going to fix a big meal today. Everyone can make their own.

Once in a while I will sit with my mother at breakfast. But every time I sit down, she starts telling me to do this or do that. She started in when I sat down with her this morning. But I told her if I couldn't sit down and relax, I wasn't going to sit there. So you escape from room to room and find something to do.

Before mother moved in, she complained that I didn't call her every day, that I didn't see her every day. Now that she's in the house, we're right back to that. Like this morning, she said she hadn't seen me all day yesterday. I said, "Well, I saw you." Sally had made her breakfast. I made her lunch and fixed her dinner. But I don't have to sit with her all day. That's what I refuse to do.

At least, my family and I have been able to talk things over. Before, it was like everyone was upset and everyone was mad, and nobody would sit down and talk about it. But now we do sit down and talk. When we were on vacation, we decided that we had to go back to living our lives the way we were living them before. The relationship between John and me is just fine now. We're geting away. We've stopped listening to my mother. And if we have a dinner party or something like that, the kids aren't at the table and neither is my mother. Whereas before, if we had friends over, everybody was included. We just give my mother her dinner earlier and that's it.

Although the physical burden of caring for my mother

has decreased, the emotional stress has increased. I'm getting nervous, depressed, tired. I could sleep 12 hours a day now. And it's not a physical tired. It's mental fatigue. I've also gained about 15 pounds.

You know, she's not really sick, but if it comes to a point where I can't take care of her, of course, she's going to have to go some place else. It's very, very hard to say, "We don't want you here." It's that old guilty feeling. Everyone knows there's child abuse. We've all heard about that. But when people get older, there's that kind of abuse, too. I keep wondering, "Am I abusing my mother?" The articles you read say it doesn't have to be physical abuse. There's also mental abuse.

John and I both think we need professional counseling. But it's my decision when to make the call — when to make the appointment. It's been hard to make decisions. Not only about this, but about other things, too. But I'll make the call, just as soon as John doesn't have to appear in court so often.

I'm not ready to give up my family and everything yet! I'm going to keep on fighting against that!

IT TAKES A LOT OF LOVE

It was 12 years of pure hell for Mae Johnson — the years of her mother's physical and mental decline. Despite the illness of her own husband, there was a period when Mae commuted weekly to her mother's home in another state to help out her elderly stepfather. When Mae's stepfather was brutally murdered, the care of her mother fell solely on Mae.

This is a story of devotion, frustration, commitment, and exhaustion — yet a story of the endurance of faith and love.

Even though it all happened two years ago, it's still very fresh and very hard for me to remember — the murder of my stepfather and the death of my mother.

My mother and dad were both in religious work. She was an Eastern Star and a state lecturer, and he was a Baptist minister. They were well known and well liked. Mother and dad were always busy and active, and they traveled a lot until their later years. Mother's health went first, so naturally dad cut down on some of his activities and travel to look after her.

Arthritis was my mother's big problem. She also had high blood pressure, because she tended to be short and fat. And she loved all of the things she shouldn't have. Mother had had surgery twice — major surgery. Back in the forties, she had had a tumor removed, but she came through that just beautifully. The second time she had surgery was several years ago. It was emergency surgery for diverticulitis. And that was horrendous! Mother was well up into her eighties at the time, so it was more or less down hill from then on.

From the time she was about 71 until the day she died, she might have had two or three good years. She didn't have a serious heart problem, but what with the wear and tear on her heart, the arthritis, the diverticulitis, which would flare up without notice, and a hip that was being ground away, mother was regularly in and out of the hospital.

When I would hear that she was in the hospital, I would take the next bus out of here. I always kept bus fare in the house, because I would never know when I was going to have to go to Alabama. After she would get out of the hospital, I would stay for four or five days or a week or ten days or more. Then when she seemed to be all right, I would come back home, because my husband is here.

Sometimes my husband would go with me, but he was working most of the time. He was supporting me and I was partially supporting my mother and dad. So usually, we couldn't both leave at the same time. But sometimes he would drive me and sometimes he would come there and get me, because he didn't want me to drive by myself. It was not always convenient for someone else to go with me. Although my aunt — my stepfather's sister — wanted to go with me, she couldn't travel because she was getting older and weaker.

My dad's health wasn't the best either at that time. But he was one of those tall, silent, "I'm not going to complain," types. He was the oldest child in a large family. And you know, then boys didn't cry. Men didn't cry and they didn't give in to their feelings. That's the way he lived and that's the way he died. In spite of his own health, though, his greatest concern was for my mother. When she was in the hospital, he would be there every day. Somtimes twice a day. I think he loved my mother very much.

Having had so many illnesses, and having been first lady of the church, mother was accustomed to having what she wanted — *when she wanted it*! And she usually wanted it yesterday. I always gave in to her, because I never wanted to cause her tears. (I had given her quite a few of those when I was young.) When I found she had the problem with her heart, I began to give in to her even more. Many times I would be opposed to what she wanted to do, but I would do it anyway. My dad also gave in to her a lot. And the church members made a baby of her. Mother was thoroughly spoiled.

Often when mother and dad were going through a crisis, or just getting on each other's nerves, I would go up and get her and keep her with me for two or three weeks or a month. This went on for years. Sometimes when dad was trying to muddle through something, mother would have one view and he would have another. And I believe that many times he felt that if he were just left alone he could think it through. Because he was very, very old school, women did not tell him what to do. Also, being a public servant gets a little much sometimes — dealing with all those people. That was very hard work and very time-involving. A lot of times, I felt like mother needed a rest. So I'd talk to my dad about it and he'd say, "Yeh, I think she deserves one. Come and get her."

Many's the time it was difficult for me to take care of her, because she would get angry with me. For example, I'd fix her food and set it on the table. Of course, that's the time she would elect to go to the bathroom. Naturally, when she came back, the food was cold. I knew all of this was some sort of punishment, but I never really knew what I was being punished for, but I was being punished. I sometimes think that she resented the fact that our roles were reversed. I think that's what it was.

Another time when she was down here she had to go to the hospital. And her doctor, whom she adored, put her on a diet. So I fixed her food exactly the way the doctor said to do it. When I put it before her, mother said, "I can't eat that." And I said, "But this is what your doctor said you could have." When my mother went back home, she told all of my friends that I had her on a diet of bread and water. She told them that that was all she was allowed to have.

Sometimes when she was down here, she was fairly rational; other times not. On one occasion, she got very angry at me. She had wanted to cash a check on the day we were going to the hairdresser. I'd take her with me, and we'd get our hair done at the same time. Now the hairdresser is in the opposite direction from where I bank. So I said, 'Mother, we can't cash the check today, because we're going to get our hair done. You give it to me, and I'll take it tomorrow, which will be more convenient, because I have to go to the bank." She didn't say anything, but I noticed her face drop. So we went to the hairdresser, came back, and had dinner. And we had a fairly quiet evening.

The next morning I got up, fixed her breakfast, put it before her, and was making tracks to get out of here to go to work. So I said, "Mother, do you want to give me your check and I will cash it today?" When I said that, she started tearing the check up. And oh, did she have words with me. I was treating her like a child. She had no control over her life — and this and that and the other thing. I just looked at her and I said, "Well now sweetheart, you are not hurting me by tearing your check up. I explained it all to you yesterday."

She was so angry that she called up my dad and told him to come and get her. He tried to soothe her over the telephone. And because he had a limited license and could only drive in the city, he didn't come that day. Mother had a pattern. As soon as she got mad with me, she wanted to go home. As soon as she got mad with him, she wanted to come here. When she wanted to leave, she'd call him up two or three times a day. She called him up the next day, and by this time, she was very angry. So I said, "While you're talking to him, tell him you tore up the check." Well, I guess she told him and she apparently told him also that I had taken her money away from her, which, of course, I hadn't. Anyway, he came the next day or so, with a friend of his, to take her home. Now she knew and I knew and, in fact, we all knew that my stepfather loved money. And if you wanted him to move, you said something about money.

I heard later that my stepfather had told several people — including the minister who drove with him — that I had taken

mother's money away from her. I think he told them that because he was trying to get someone to drive him here and what
mother said would make the trip to get his wife more urgent. I
don't believe that deep down he really thought I took that
money.

Well, I've never taken a quarter from my mother in my life.
But you know, somebody's always going to believe something
like that. I don't care what you say, they do. A couple of my
friends got into arguments over it. And one said, "That's not
so. I've known her all of my life and she's never done that.
She's always been good to her mother. I know she didn't do
that!"

There was a period of several months that I was spending
three days a week there and four days here, trying to do what
needed to be done. Because my dad was so concerned about
my mother, he would sometimes not even open the mail. He
knew that when I came, I would open the mail and tell him
what was happening and whom he owed. Often, I would write
the checks.

By the time I got back the next week, some of these things
would have been taken care of. If not, I would push until we
got them done. My father was very stubborn and he didn't
have a lot of formal education, which was another handicap.
He was the type of man who didn't want to be told anything.
He always wanted to take care of things himself. I'm sure you
know the type. It's always difficult to deal with someone who
has the handicap of a lesser education, I always felt I had to be
very careful dealing with him because he was not my father, he
was my stepfather. But he raised me and I had the utmost respect for him and a great deal of affection for him. Even so, I
didn't want to do anything that would have created a "Your
child did *this*" or "*Your* child said *that*" kind of situation. So I
leaned over backwards to keep peace and harmony in the
house.

Mother's mind started getting bad, I would say, roughly

five years before she died. She would have her good days and her bad days. And as it got worse and worse, I spoke to her doctor about it. In fact, each time I went there, I conferred with him about my fears and asked him questions. Up until that time, she'd had small lapses — like we all have — and we'd just say, "She's getting a little senile, which is to be expected."

I've always heard that someone in her condition turns on the persons nearest them. So my stepfather and I got most of the brunt of it. Other people would walk into the house or into her hospital room and she would be pleasant and smiling and talking. On the other hand, dad and I might be sitting there and she wouldn't say anything at all. Friends would come into her room when I was picking up her lunch dishes with the food she'd left on them and they'd say, "Baby are you hungry? Do you want to eat?" She'd say, "Yes," like she hadn't had anything to eat at all. Just like a kid. I didn't let that bother me. It hurt, but I couldn't let it bother me because I could see the other signs.

Well I got used to that, finally, and some of my friends got used to it too. But there were others who probably thought I didn't feed her. I don't know, and at this point, I don't care. I got to the point where I just did not care what people talked about, because I knew what I was doing. Those who really knew me, knew what I was doing, too. But I don't know what my mother thought I was doing. I know she loved me very much. And I think that if she had been her normal self, she wouldn't have said or done some of the things she did. I think it was a case of her mind deteriorating.

When I would come back to Alabama after having been home for a few days, mother would always seem to be glad to see me. She wouldn't say anything, but her eyes would light up when she saw me. The deterioration of her mind was just something we were going to have to deal with. I think that she had a lot of suppressed anger in her. I don't know whether it was against my dad, against me, against life. But I believe that anger and maybe frustration had something to do with her behavior. Being a public servant — which she was as a minister's wife for so many years — is a very, very hard job.

My stepfather did talk to me about the problem. I was up there once when she was in, what I would call, moderate health. One night, she became suicidal. She was angry and frustrated and she had a knife. My dad liked to fish and hunt, so he had knives and guns and things like that around the house. We struggled for the knife and I took it away from her. Then she went up and got an antique pistol that my father had. It was one of those guns with a long barrel, and I didn't even know whether it would shoot or not.

Next, she decided to go outside — it was November, I think, and she had on a chiffon gown and robe. When I realized what she was going to do, I said, "You shouldn't go out this time of night, somebody could hit you over the head." She said, "I hope somebody does." Mother started for the door, so I reached for her. She pulled away and I tackled her. Now mother was shorter and heavier than I am, so we both ended up on the floor. After I pulled her out of reach of the doorknob, I called my dad, who was upstairs in bed. When he came to the top of the steps, my mother looked over her shoulder and told my dad that I jumped on her. My dad said, "Oh, she didn't jump on you. She would never do anything to hurt you."

I sometimes think that she had it in her mind to do away with him. And that's when I really began to pay attention to a lot of the little things that I began to put together. She had stored up anger against him, and possibly against me, because it seemed to her that we were managing her life and not letting her make any decisions. Well, it had come to the point where we didn't think she was capable of making the best decisions for herself.

At that time, my mother had been in and out of a nursing home as well as the hospital. My dad was always opposed to putting her in a nursing home until it became a "must." Then when she showed the slightest improvement, he'd go and snatch her out. Maybe her behavior was caused partly by some of the changes she went through going from home to nursing home and back home. It was very hard on all three of us. I'm sure mother must have suffered greatly. She had this arthritis for years, and she would be almost crazy with pain.

In the spring of '82, my mother and dad's house was almost completely demolished by fire. My mother was in the hospital at the time and my father was displaced — boarding out, you know — until the contractor finished rebuilding the house. Although it was not really finished, my dad moved back in in August. The church members did not want him to move in. But you know how it is when you have a home and you want to be in it. So he moved in before it was finished. I can understand his feelings.

This was at the time that the insurance company was paying off on the house. The money was going to the bank into two or three different accounts, namely my dad's and the contractor's. One day, the talk of the town was that the last insurance payment was being made to my dad. Now, my dad knew just about everybody in town and everybody knew him. In a sense, he had helped raise all the children in the town. Since everyone knew my dad and since he was not going to do any harm to anybody, he didn't feel anybody would do harm to him. Nobody would do any harm to him because he was an elderly man and he had lived there for such a long, long time. I really don't know how old my dad was then. To tell the truth, I don't think he even knew how old he was. He was supposed to be about 94. But you know, back when he was born, they didn't record black births. "Oh, child, I know when he was born 'cause so and so's cow had a calf that day."

The evening the insurance check had come, a young man my father had baptized came down to the house and asked to talk to my father. Knowing the young man and his family, my dad let him in. The young man, who was out of work, wanted to talk about his domestic problems. He also wanted to borrow some money. The young man evidently thought there was a large sum of money in the house because of the insurance check. Now my stepfather was sometimes careless with money and he was a very generous and openhanded man — until he found out that you were just trying to use him. Evidently, this young man already owed him some money, and my dad was not letting him have any more. So he killed him.

Later that evening, the young man was seen driving my dad's car. Now no one sat under the wheel of that car except my dad or myself or the young man who regularly drove for him when his eyesight began failing. Naturally, someone questioned the boy about driving my dad's car. "What are you doing driving the Reverend's car?" The boy said, "The Reverend told me to get the car filled up with gas." Now that wasn't so, and the person knew it, because dad would always have the other young man gas up the car if he didn't do it himself. Because he knew that the person who had seen him in dad's car would mention it, the young man and his two accomplices took the car to an isolated area and burned it.

The mother of the boy who murdered my dad was the person that I had been paying to look after my mother. And she had been as faithful as any daughter could have been. One time when my mother came out of the hospital, this woman took her into her own home. At the time, my own husband was in the hospital here in the city, so I couldn't go up and be with my mother. This woman fed my mother, bathed her, and got the doctor for her when she needed him. To tell the truth, I loved that woman. And the boy had helped her look after my mother during the six or eight weeks mother was in her home. When my mother needed to be lifted, the boy would help.

When I first started receiving calls about my father's death, the callers would not tell me who did it, although everyone knew. One person finally told me. When I heard, I felt as bad for that mother as I felt for myself. Her son was 26 years old. He had a wife and children and was out of a job. I also understand that he had a drug habit. And when you're on drugs, you're not yourself.

I don't hate the boy, but I don't love him, because he didn't have to kill the old man. When the boy voluntarily confessed, he told police that my father had said, "Don't kill me because I don't have any money. Don't kill me." But he did it anyway. I feel sorry for his wife and their babies. One of the babies — a son — was born while he was in jail awaiting trial. It was just a heartbreaking thing all around, as I figure it. Whatever happened to the boy was not going to bring my stepfather back. Even so, I just can't feel bad toward his mother and the rest of his family. He was an adult and he was responsible for his own actions. I'm trying to forgive him. It's hard, but I'm trying. It was just a terrible, terrible tragedy. It wasn't the baby's fault — I bought the baby clothes — it wasn't his wife's fault, it wasn't his mother's fault. I dearly loved his mother because she took such good care of my mother.

It was a while before I even told my mother about my dad's death. The doctor had said, "It's up to you to tell her, and you pick the time." Well, she was in the hospital facing more surgery, and I didn't want her told until I thought she was strong enough to take it. After all, she couldn't go to the funeral. My husband couldn't come to the funeral either, because he was in the hospital himself.

Someone else did tell mother about dad's death. I was very angry about that and I still am. Somebody in the church, thinking she was doing her good deed, went up to the hospital and told her. I didn't know that. Afterwards when I went to visit mother, she would just look at me. She wouldn't say anything to me. Finally, mother said to a good friend of mine, "Nobody's telling me anything." Of course, she was talking about me. Well, it was breaking my heart not telling her, but I didn't know what effect it would have on her — facing surgery as she was.

I didn't tell her about dad until after the surgery was over and they were ready to send her home. Then I said, "Mother, the doctor says that you will be going home in a few days. But when you go home, somebody will be missing." She knew, of course, it was my dad. When I told her, she just turned her head and started to cry. She never once said anything to me about waiting to tell her, even though she had said to one of our friends, "I know he's dead." Sometimes this bothers me so much, but I truly thought I was doing what was best for her at the time.

When they sent mother home from the hospital, they sent nurses in to train me to look after her. And I stayed there — with the exception of a few trips home — for the next six months. Many people were advising me to pull up stakes and move there. And maybe, had she lived, I would have been compelled to do so. I just don't know how long I would have been able to go on living in two places. I couldn't manage it financially.

When mother had been home a couple of months, I called the doctor one night to tell him she had developed a cough. As it turned out, it was pneumonia. He said to meet him at the hospital at eight o'clock the next morning. What bothered me about this was that I had tried to keep her covered and keep her temperature normal. And I had slept on the same floor with her until she began to get stronger and better. In the morning, the doctor said to me, "These things happen. It's not negligence on your part. They get pneumonia. I just don't think it was anything you did, because she was kept clean, she was kept dry, and the house was comfortable. So you don't need to feel guilty." But I did. And sometimes I still do. But when we brought her home from the hospital, the doctor came through and he said, "You're doing a good job. There's nothing here that would make me think that your mother is not getting proper care."

When mother had to go back to the hospital with pneumo-

nia, it seemed that she had just sort of given up. She stayed in
the hospital for quite some time — 31 days, I think. At the end
of her time in the hospital, the doctors said, "When she leaves
here, she'll be going into a nursing home, because you just
cannot handle her. You do not have the equipment at home."
What they meant was that I didn't have the proper tools if anything serious developed. I did have the ordinary equipment at
home — you know, the electric bed, the bed table, a wheelchair, a commode, and all of that. Whatever they told me she
needed, I got. And I could rent it, which is what I did, because
I never felt a permanency there. My husband didn't like Alabama, my aunt didn't like Alabama. I'm my aunt's sole kin.
I'm all she's got in the world. So if I was going to move there, I
would have to uproot everybody and make everybody unhappy. I had talked to the hospital's social service department
about transferring mother to the city but then, she got
pneumonia.

So we moved her from the hospital to a nursing home
again. This was the second nursing home she had been in. It
was very clean and very cheerful. But it was not home. So your
heart feels like a rock in your bosom. The help were cheerful
and cooperative and they did everything for her. They fed her,
because she had stopped eating. They pumped all of the muc-
ous out of her lungs. And it was just awful. She never seemed
to fully recover from that pneumonia.

In January, I came back home to see my husband. He was
coming out of the hospital, I think. I wasn't home very long
but what they called from Alabama and said I had better come
back. I got there Sunday afternoon and went straight from the
bus station to the nursing home. I spent some time with
mother and then went to a friend's house for dinner. I went
home and went to bed. It seemed like mother was just waiting
for me to come back, because about one o'clock in the morning
the phone rang. I knew exactly what it was. So I got dressed
and went back to the nursing home and spent a little

called the undertaker from there. I don't know how I made it, but I'm thankful I did.

During the last year or two of dad's life — whenever mother was in the hospital or nursing home — he kept saying, "She's coming home. She's really coming back home." He became so obsessed with that that he neglected to do a number of things that he should have done. The property taxes were delinquent, for example. And, as a result, there were a lot of things that I, as an only child, had to take care of.

There was no will, and everything was a complete mess! With my stepfather passing first, his estate had to be closed. But before it could get closed, she was gone. He had passed everything on to her and, eventually, I guess it will come to me. My stepdad had a son, from a previous marriage, that no one had seen for 29 years. And from what my attorney was able to find out, his son is probably dead.

My stepdad wasn't close to the rest of his family either. His father, who was not very nice to him, pulled him out of school and made him go to work. His education certainly didn't prosper from that. Because he was going to night school when he and my mother were married, she had him on one side with his homework and me on the other side with my homework. My stepdad was one of a very large family and when he began getting ahead, some of his brothers and sisters began to resent him. They were not really a close family.

Everything was such a muddle after my mother died. Thank God, I had the family lawyer. He's an honest, kind, compassionate man. He has answered every question — idiotic as it may have seemed — that I ever asked him. I'm down to the wire now, and I think I have cleared up almost everything. But it's been something to keep me awake nights. And doing this has kept me broke. I think if his son had come in and given me some part of the money I had spent, I would have signed everything over to him. There have been many times when I wanted to give it all up, but I couldn't, because my mother and stepfather had worked too hard for what they had. The estate is in probate now and I think it's coming out all right. I would love to go away for a while and forget everything. But I want all of this behind me. I don't want to carry it with me.

It's been almost two years since dad died. Mother died about six months later. I didn't expect my mother to live much longer than my dad. They had been married for so long that they were just like limbs for each other. What's more, I think they loved each other very much.

And what about my own marriage during that terrible time? Well, I was worried about that, too. I knew my husband didn't want to live in Alabama. But whenever I had to go there, my husband would say, "Well, if you must, you must." The two of us have been through a lot together and he's always hung in there. I was living a soap opera. It was incredible the way things kept unfolding — one thing after another, and all bad! I couldn't have gotten through these past years without my husband. I've gotten through them now, and I thank God. He's been good to me. One thing, he's given me a gem of a husband.

In thinking over these past years, I realize it takes a lot of love and patience to take care of a loved one who's physically and mentally deteriorating. You have to be patient with all of the changes that are taking place in that person. When my crises were going on, it would help when friends would tell me of similar experiences they were having with their parents. Sometimes, you just feel like screaming and tearing your hair and walking the wind. But you can't. Most of the time when I felt that way, I would go out into the yard and stay there for a while. Sometimes it would get to a point where one friend would call another friend and say, "Go down and sit with Mother Williams, I'm gonna take Mae for a ride. We're going shopping or something." Mother was *never* left alone during the months that I was with her after my dad died.

As I said, it takes a great deal of love and patience, a lot of good friends, and a great deal of prayer to keep you from losing your grip.

THE SIX-YEAR TREADMILL

When Joan Bradley's mother-in-law gave up her independence to move into a nursing home, life and lifestyle changed dramatically for the Bradleys. Conflicts of interests and concerns emerged as Joan and her husband, Don, readjusted their busy professional lives and schedules to accommodate Nana's new life. The regular visits to the nursing home, the logistics of arranging an outing for Nana, the production of seeing that she got to and from family events, and the constant concern for her health and well being created a six-year treadmill for the Bradleys. But it's over now, and Joan and Don won't have to visit that nursing home any more.

"I wish she were dead! I wish she would die!" I can't tell you how many times I thought that when she was in the nursing home. She was taking away from *my* life because of the need for my husband to be with her . . . to spend time with her . . . and to think about her. The whole thing was difficult for me. I don't know how other people in my situation handle it. But I know it was hard for me.

I guess it was the fact that my mother-in-law was in a nursing home that disturbed me the most. Before going into a nursing home, Nana had moved from a two-story house of her own — the family moved her — to a retirement village, where she had her own little townhouse, but took her meals in a central location. And the place was managed and cared for. She was doing fine there. It was in the suburbs and it was an excellent place. But they don't take care of anyone who gets sick. The minute you get sick, they literally ship you out.

The priest and nuns, I don't care who they are — what religious order or whatever — are very avaricious when it comes to a situation like that. "This person can't be taken care of here. We can't afford *not* to have someone else in here, someone who can pay the rent and take care of themselves. We don't want the responsibility." Well, nobody wants the responsibility. You don't. I don't. My husband doesn't. His sister doesn't. Her husband doesn't. The church doesn't. Hospitals don't — and *won't.* So what are you left with? These warehouses!

The failure of Nana's eyesight was the predominant reason why my husband and his sister finally decided she had to go to a nursing home. She had become less and less able to take care of herself. And she got to the point where she could not function on her own. Blindness was the problem. It was then that I had my first introduction to the wonderful world of nursing homes. And I found that if they didn't stink with urine, you know you're not in the right place. They're just terrible.

Nana absolutely loathed and detested the nursing home. "Why did you put me here?" "Why have *you* put me here?" she blamed the family. Well, they *did* put her there. No matter how much it was explained to her that she couldn't see well enough to take care of herself — that she couldn't cook her breakfast, that she couldn't do for herself — she wanted to go back and live in her own home. "I was doing fine there. My meals were taken care of." And so on. Well, she was making a cup of tea and burning every pot in the place when she tried to boil water. Nana never tried to make us feel guilty about not taking her in, however. She never made any such remarks to me, anyway. She may have to Don's sister; I don't know. But she didn't to me.

Idealistically, at least, it seemed to me that one of us could have taken her into our home. Taking care of her ourselves would have saved all that money and would have made her happier too. Well, that's Pollyanna. I found out later that there were many people like us who did not know that taking in the older parent was not necessarily the best decision. But it seemed like a good idea to me.

Of course, it was a good idea, if it were not my home. I was talking about his sister's home. A woman who did not have a job, such as I did, was home during the day, and had plenty of help. "Why doesn't that happen?" I asked myself. Why? Then at least *I* wouldn't have to see all those people in the nursing home when I went — which I hated! I think I hated that more . . .feared that more than anything else. That particular smell. There's nothing like it. They say hospitals have a smell. Well, the one I work in doesn't have it, or I'm so used to it I don't notice. But nursing homes *do* have a smell. And it's the smell of hopelessness and fear. I hate it!

I always did wonder why Laurel didn't take Nana into her home. She had plenty of room and plenty of help. But I think she just didn't want the daily responsibility. Even if Laurel had generously agreed to take Nana in, we would have had a whole new series of problems. Because it wouldn't work out. Laurel would be on the phone saying, "I have Nana to take care of, you're going to have to help me out. You're going to have to do this and that." So it really would have been the same.

I remember in my childhood, my grandparents had a large family — nine children. Six of the nine just could not accept any of the responsibility for my grandparents, leaving it to the other three. So it doesn't matter how large or small the family is, if you don't have agreement about what you're going to do. My grandparents did end up staying with someone in the family. And the rest of those who were interested enough contributed toward the care.

It would have been devastating for Nana in our home. I'm sure of that. And I supposed a nursing home is the next best thing. But you had better be able to afford it. Or forget it! It is really astronomically expensive. I'm talking about $3,000 a month, *minimum*. That doesn't count the drugs or the doctor's visits or the special visits from the social worker, which are all charged to you also. It's a shame, though, to think of working all your life and raising a family and then having your life savings eaten up by your last days, so to speak — your last years.

As a matter of fact, Nana *did* live with us for a while. I guess I wanted to block this out. We thought it would be great for the children to have Nana around and great for Nana to have the children around. This was right before Nana went into her retirement village. At that time, we were fighting to maintain the existing situation as long as we possibly could. But when she was living with us, Nana would sit in the living room, waiting for us to come home at the end of the day. When Don came home or when he and I met after working all day, Nana expected to be served a drink and she expected that we would talk with her. Well, we had things to say to each other. So we'd go out in the kitchen to have a little conversation. And before long, you know, shuffle, shuffle, out she'd come. And I thought to myself, "This is never going to work." And it didn't in the long run. I *really had* blocked this whole episode out.

Originally I went on nursing home visits with Don's sister — to find the right place for Nana. And I resented that, too, because I hated going into all of those places where these terribly sick people were — and it wasn't my own mother, even. It was my husband's mother. "Why wasn't he there, instead of me?" I'd ask myself. Well, I never did get the answer to that. Maybe I never asked the question.

When Nana went into the nursing home, everything changed. It became a different situation. When she was healthy and full of fun, it was a pleasure to spend time with her. Now, she wasn't functioning well. She wasn't seeing well. Her mind was beginning to go. And it was now a chore to visit her. Something we had taken for granted before — visiting our parents — now became a chore. It was because Nana was growing older and it was frightening just to see it happen. Not only to see it happen to someone else, but even worse to realize that it's going to happen to you. "What's going to happen to me?" I thought. "Are my kids going to feel this way about me as I do about Nana? I'll bet they are. They'll say they're not going to. But they're going to. I know it.

Trying to — how do I want to put this — but trying to put on a good face, a smiling face, was hard. There was no more being straight with Nana once she was in the nursing home, getting iller by the day. There was no more telling her anything. She couldn't remember half of what she'd been told or else she misinterpreted it. You couldn't say some things to her — at least I couldn't. I didn't feel comfortable. This person, who had been my husband's mother — and notice I said "*had been*" — now was somebody else. Somebody interfering in my life, interfering in my personal life. In my professional life it was because we were always looking for a better nursing home. And because I worked in a hospital, it was up to me to talk to the social service people who would tell me the best nursing homes. I didn't want that responsibility. It was not my mother to begin with, but even worse, what if I made a mistake? What if I recommended a nursing home that was the wrong one, and they said, "Joan said so." Well, I didn't want that responsibility.

I found myself resenting both Nana and the situation. I think I resented the situation, primarily, and resented Nana as a product of the situation. There was never a sense of complete freedom when we were planning any family event, for example. It always was, "And then there's Nana." Nana was a problem for almost half of our married life, a preoccupation to a certain degree. Not a daily preoccupation, but a weekly one and probably more often than that, because there was always the planning required. If I wanted to have someone over on a Sunday — "What time can I do this?" I guess it wouldn't have mattered — or shouldn't have mattered — but it mattered greatly. I resented that particular hindrance to my schedule. I sound cold and heartless, but it bothered me. Why couldn't things be normal? And spontaneous?

In order to get Nana ready to go out, you had to call the nursing home at a certain time of day and preferably the day before. You had to go out there and lay out her clothes. Someone had to do that. If the nursing home did that, she would end up with the wrong shoes, with the wrong dress, or some damn thing. If *you* didn't care, *they* didn't care. Nana's outings became productions.

As I said, Nana's main problem was her eyesight. She had no peripheral vision. She had tunnel vision. She could see directly in front of her, but, of course, she would have to turn her head to get the side vision. When Nana went to the first nursing home, she had a cane so that she could walk around. Now this evaluation as to whether you have a cane or not is all in the hands of the authorities who run the nursing home. The social workers and these other people — people I can't stand, anyway. When she moved to the second nursing home, the decision was made that she didn't *need* a cane — that she could just figure out for herself how to get around. The decision was made. It's not what I want, what my husband wants, what his sister wants, what his mother wants. She *did not need* a cane. She could get by. Well, she *did* get by, yes. She still kept wandering around. But this was just one example of the powerlessness of people in nursing homes and of their families.

During the six years that Nana was in the nursing home, everything revolved around her, so to speak. It seemed like any family event — certainly any major family event — was affected by who was picking Nana up at the nursing home and who was driving her back. And people, meaning Laurel and Don, tried to decide between them how to get out of doing it, because it was a chore. I supposed they also had feelings of resentment, feelings of powerlessness, feelings of guilt. I'm sure they had feelings of frustration, definitely. Certainly feelings of guilt, which I think are inevitable in a situation like this.

I think the older person creates guilt by his or her very existence. It's a horrible thing to say, but with many people, I think it's true. Nana did not have the psychic pain. It took a toll more on others. Laurel ran herself ragged. She would be there two or three times a day. That's super guilt. Laurel always said that Don would really be upset when Nana died because he didn't do enough.

We went to visit Nana once a week, *minimum*. I mean *once a week, minimum*. I think that's an awful lot of time. When you're working full time, you spend all day Saturday doing your errands, Sunday you visit the nursing home, and then Monday it's back to the office. When we went to the nursing home, we stayed as long as we could tolerate it, which would be about an hour . . . an hour and fifteen minutes . . . or an hour and a half.

Nana was always glad to see us. And she always said she hadn't seen us in months and months, which used to frost us because we had been there just the week before. Obviously, she wasn't aware of that, which made you wonder what in hell you were doing there in the first place. I remember one Sunday saying to Don, when he just didn't feel like going to the nursing home, "Don't worry, Nana won't know it anyway. She always says we haven't been there for a month. So what difference does it make?" He didn't say much to that. He went, of course.

A lot of visiting in the nursing home, I think, is guilt being assuaged. It's an appointment with destiny, so to speak. "Now I'll do this, and I'll be okay. It won't happen to me." I really believe that. Really, after you're an adult, you don't go visit your mother once a week. Good lord, I don't see my kids but once or twice a year. Well, my daughter, who is in town, maybe once every six weeks.

And if nursing homes were what they're cracked up to be — or what they say they are — in terms of activities and involvement with people who are able to be involved and active, then they wouldn't have time to see you because they would be too busy. But they're not. It's disgusting. And the bucks they're getting for that is just incredible.

Nana always seemed to be about the same when we went to see her. She was more animated on some days than she was on others. By and large, she accepted her fate, even though she railed against it. When she came to visit, she would say, "Oh this is such a treat. We haven't done this in years." We'd say, "That's right." She may not have wanted to go back to the home, but she never said she didn't. Underneath it all, I think Nana was very sad. She didn't complain a lot about it, but when we would be leaving after a visit with her, it became very poignant. She didn't cry, I'll give her that, but she was very pathetic. "Do you have to go? You just got here." To her, perhaps so. To us, it was an hour of torment or an hour-and-a-half. Often her hair was not fixed nicely and sometimes she smelled like she hadn't been bathed in a long time. She had a bath once a week, you see. She also had her hair done once a week. And the hairdresser, I guess, didn't do it the way she wanted it.

The relationship between Nana and her son and daughter changed certainly from what it was years ago. When she began to become ill and we realized she couldn't keep her house, everything was taken out of her control, in terms of her where-withal, finances, and so forth. A trust was set up. She seemed to understand this at the time and she didn't really seem to resent it. Well, yes, she did resent it in the sense that she would complain she didn't have any money. We'd leave her a couple of dollars or a five dollar bill or something and we'd come back and say, "What did you buy with your money?" And she'd say, "What money? It's gone. *They stole it.*" They, meaning the help, you know. Well, that didn't seem possible, but then. . .

Then we'd say, "See why we don't leave you any money?" But she'd say she needed carfare. She was going down town and she had to have money to get on the streetcar. She was going to meet so and so for lunch. Well, so and so was a person who was probably no longer around. In that case, we would give her a couple of bucks and we'd never know whatever happened to it. But she didn't like it. She didn't like it at all. She was the one who had dispensed money for years, and now it was being dispensed to her.

We'd never argue with her. At least Don would never argue with her. He'd always say, "Isn't that nice?" And that would be the end of it. Whereas his sister took a different approach. She demanded that Nana stay in reality. In doing it, she would say to her, "What coat did you wear? What streetcar did you take? What number was it?" Well, Laurel thought she was keeping Nana in reality and not letting her slip into this senility bag. I didn't agree with that. I thought Don's approach was better. When Laurel did this, Nana would become more argumentative, insisting she was right. So I think that the approach was wrong. Laurel and I just didn't agree about that, that's all.

I felt obliged to join in the weekly visits, even though it was not my mother. It was Don's mother. And I didn't particularly care to expose myself to that particular pain. It was painful for me. And so I would dream up reasons not to be able to go. And Don got resentful. He'd say, "Of course, you're trying to get out of going to see Nana," and I'd say, "Yes, I am." And I'd say, "If you were half way honest, you'd say you would like to get out of it too." Of course, he'd just become madder and walk out the door and go. The end result was that I'd quit not going. I decided it was cheaper emotionally for me to go.

I always felt Nana was a sweet person — sort of a nice little old lady. And she accepted me and I accepted her. I had no positive or negative feelings. It was very neutral. More positive than negative, of course. I could get affectionate toward her. My children loved her. That is, the boys did. They thought she was just dynamite. Of course, she did have a great sense of humor. And she always liked to be a child. And of course the kids loved to be like that too. And even though they were adults, they liked to be children with Nana.

I think the whole problem of people getting too old so that they are not able to care for themselves is a painful one for every member of the family. I don't care who it is. You'd think that the person who is the spouse would not be as involved. If it were my mother, I would be real involved. But now I'm real involved, and it isn't even my mother. That's the thing that used to drive me bananas. I'd say to myself, "What is this bullshit? How come I'm so taken into this?"

There definitely is a stigma to the nursing home. Everyone of these people walking into that nursing home on Sunday afternoon is there out of guilt, I swear to God. They certainly don't look happy. They don't look as though they're there for fun, fun, fun. Emotionally, that is. And I think to myself, "I hope my kids never put me in one." They might. I couldn't take it. Well, I've made a pact with a friend of mine. I said she and I would never have that happen to us. We'd be bag ladies before we'd end up like that. And this pact was not made in jest. At least being a bag lady would be exciting. But to live in a nursing home would be the pits. I couldn't stand it.

It's funny that we go through life in such a weird way. We work and slave really to provide for our kids and then just as we get rid of our kids — when they're off on their own — along comes the sick mother or the sick mother-in-law or the sick father. Now you've taken care of one generation — the one coming up that's now been launched as well as its going to be — and you turn around and think, "Now it's time for me." But no, no time for you, because we have to take care of the old people now. Before you know it, we're going to be old. And we'll not have had time for ourselves.

Nana was ready to move again. We had been looking at new places. As a matter of fact, I just went to the doctor and got the names of a whole bunch of new places. Nana was always set to move, to find a new place. Each time, she thought it would be better. Hope sprang eternal for her that it would be a nicer place. Really, I do not know the answer. It wouldn't have been ideal in our home. It wouldn't have been ideal at Laurel's either. And it wouldn't have been ideal for Nana to spend six months at one house and six months at the other. We thought of that.

On the other hand, Nana didn't seem to have too many friends at the nursing home. She had some friends for a while. She started out in a double room because the nursing home staff said she would be better off not being by herself. She never liked her roommates, however. She didn't get along with her roommates, so they put her in a four-bed room. And she seemed to do better there, because she wasn't interacting one-on-one. But she never became close to anybody. She never said to us, "I want you to meet my friend . . . ." She just didn't seem to have any friends. And I don't know what the reason for that was. I really don't.

Outside the nursing home she had many friends and still does — or did — I should say. Friends were able to stop, pick her up, and take her out. She had a set of people who were taking her out in addition to us. Mainly it was childhood friends. They would take her out to dinner. They were very kind to her. They were very open and loving with her. It was nice.

Life in the nursing home was not all bad for her. For her, life never was. She never had to worry about a thing in her whole life. By that I mean, she married very well, and she always had plenty of money. She had the best medical care in the world. She had the best nursing home on the north side — maybe second best. Second most expensive. She didn't have to be concerned about anything. Nana sailed through life. Sailed through life, indeed. Blithely on her way.

Nana was relatively lucid up until the day she surprised us all and died — going from what I considered not even being ill. It's funny. You become calloused. I became calloused. I should say it that way. When an older person complains of heart murmurs, you say, "Yes, uh huh, uh huh," not believing there is anything to it. Well, fortunately, its the nurses and doctors at the nursing home, not the family, who decides on the patient's condition.

In Nana's case, she went to the hospital for palpitations of the heart. We all yawned and said, "We'll visit her when we get around to it." At least that was my attitude. "She'll be home in two days, anyhow. She always has been in the past." Well, she didn't make it.

What has happened to me since she died? First of all, her dying did come as quite a shock. We did not expect it. As I said, we thought it was just another little thing. And lo and behold, my God, she did die. Immediately I started feeling guilty, because I had wished ill of her on more than one occasion, as I mentioned earlier. I felt terrible. But that didn't last very long, because I realized that no one can wish somebody dead and have it actually work. Since then, all the lovely things about her are coming to the surface. And I am remembering all of the kind and fun things. All of the pain and all of the rest of it has gone away. Now I can't imagine not looking at Nana and saying, "Isn't she swell?" When many's the time I would look at her and think, "Get going."

I also asked myself, "Is there something I would have done differently? Is there a way I would have acted more kindly? More thoughtfully?" I really don't think so. I think the situation is so fraught with emotion and fear and all those other things that you can't be anything other than the way you are at the time.

No, in a very real and final sense, the problem has been solved. It has now been solved by the fact that this Sunday and next Sunday and all the Sundays to come, I won't have to ever go again to that terrible place, have those terrible feelings, and confront, so directly, my own mortality.

OH, TO GO FISHIN'!

For 14 years, Florence Turner cared for her invalid mother-in-law, raised her children, and worked outside the home, so she and her husband could make ends meet. What began as a joyous experience — sharing her home with her husband's· mother — became one of exhaustion, frustration, resentment, self-doubt.

In the pages that follow, Florence talks about her personal struggle, the part of her own life 'that she lost along the way, and the irony of mama's preference for her other son — a son who would not inconvenience himself or his family to share responsibility for the care of his mother.

I first met my mother-in-law by going down south and taking the baby with me. I was going to my own mother's funeral, and I had to have someone to leave the baby with. So I said, "Okay, I'll go and take her to my mother-in-law." When I got there, I found she was a darling person — a little, petite person. She was just beautiful. But all I got to know about her then was from going there, dropping the baby off, going back, picking the baby up, and sitting with her for, maybe 30 minutes to an hour. That was all the time I had with her. Afterwards, then, I got letters from her. She got somebody to write them.

It was about five years after I met her that mama came to live with us. The telephone rang about 11:30 one night, and my husband answered the phone. It was his mother. "But mama," he says, "where are you?" And she says, "I'm in Mobile." He says, "What are you doing in Mobile? You're supposed to be in Blytheville, Arkansas." She says, "I live in Mobile now. I moved here." She had been there about two months, and we didn't even know it. He says, "Who do you live with?" And she told him, "Well, I'm living with my niece.

But," she says, "I can't stay here. My arthritis is getting worse, and I'm going to have to stay with somebody." At that time, mama's youngest son was in Germany. So my husband says, "Well, you'll stay with me." She says, "No, talk it over with your wife, and then let me know." Well, my husband was so upset by the fact that she's living in Mobile, that he didn't know where she was, and hadn't heard from her in that time, he said, "No way, you just live here with us." She says, "Okay, tell you what, you put your wife on." When I got on the phone, she says, "I have arthritis and its getting worse. I can't stay by myself because now I'm getting where I can't prepare my food. Will it be an inconvenience," she says, "if I came up there and stayed with you all until maybe some other arrangements can be made?" I told her, "Sure. Come on." When I was younger, I always wanted to be a nurse — that is, until I saw a lady have a baby.

My husband went to Mobile and got mama. This was two days before Thankgiving in 1970. He got a friend of his and he got a trailer and he went to Mobile. He brought her back the day after Thanksgiving. It was about 6:30 that afternoon when they got here. And she and I talked until — I guess it was — about one or one thirty in the morning. She was telling different little things about when she was young and how it was for her when she was living in Blytheville. She was, to put it bluntly, a gossiper. She liked to gossip, and I did too. Well, I do. So she was telling me about everybody's business in town. She knew that I didn't know the people, so it didn't really matter. It was nice.

So mama moved in. The bed my husband had given me as a wedding present — I gave to her. And the whole set of bedroom furniture, too. I asked my husband if it was okay or if he would think hard of me if I did this. She didn't have a bed. She sold all of her things in Blytheville. Then she went to Mobile, so she didn't have anything much. All she had was a footlocker, a reclining chair, and some dishes. That was it. My husband

said, "Is this what you want to do?" And I said, "Yes." So I gave
her my bedroom set and the room that my husband and I were
sleeping in. Then, I told my husband, "Why, we don't need a
diningroom. We'll get a bed and put it in there. And so we took
the diningroom as a bedroom. We had two young kids, living
at home at the time, and they had a room together.

At this particular time, mama was just walking with a cane.
But her hands were in such shape that she couldn't hold a pot
— if she managed to pick it up — and you put just a cup of water in it. She couldn't pick up an iron skillet at all. It got to
where she couldn't prepare her food. And when she was living
in Blytheville, she would have all kinds of problems, because
they were still using coal. That would mean going from the
house to the outside, getting in coal and making her own fires.

After Mama came to live with us, we would sit and we
would have long conversations about things that happened
when she was a girl. It was interesting, because she told me
things, like about the Titanic and about other things in history
I knew had happened. The things happened when she was a
kid. Mama, who was born and raised on a farm, used to sit
and talk about what people used to do when she was young.
She used to talk about things they used to wear — the different
styles they used to wear. She talked about bustles. You know,
when you used to see bustles in the movies, the ladies would
wear them underneath their dresses. But mama came along at
the time when they wore them outside. And she would always
talk about how funny it was when the ladies would go to
church. The ladies would get happy — religious-wise — sing-
ing and shouting, and then they'd lose their bustles. It was real
funny the way she would tell it. She'd also tell how she would
love to ride the ferry across the river, and how you could walk
out onto part of the river when it was frozen over.

Mama was born in Kentucky, but she left Kentucky when
she was seven years old. Her most vivid memory is her life in
Mississippi. I never knew what part of Mississippi they lived

in, because I think they moved about a lot. The way she would tell it, it would have been a thrill to live back there in those days. And it would have been fun. She says she liked to fall off the ferry into the water because she was looking so hard at this huge, mammoth thing that everybody said was a whale. Somehow or other, he had gotten into the Mississippi River. I didn't believe that story too much, but it was fun hearing it.

My mother-in-law was very fair complected. She was very fair. Of course, as she got older, she started to darken up a little bit. She had experiences when she was young that a lot of us who are a darker color didn't have. There were people then that didn't recognize her and honor her as they would honor me. Because I'm darker skinned, they would honor me as somebody who would come and work in your house and then go home. But when she was a young woman, if you didn't see the difference in dress when you walked into a house where she was working, you would wonder, "Who is the lady of the house?" If you walk into a house where I'm working, you know automatically that that woman is black. Mama experienced prejudice. She wasn't bitter about any of this, because from the way she would tell it, she had led a full life — even on the farm and even with the little that they had. She had a very full, rich life.

I think mama had about eight or nine miscarriages before one of her babies lived. It lived to be about six months old and then it died. Then she had three more kids — three boys. My husband and her oldest son and then the youngest son. My husband was the middle child.

Mama and her husband lived on a plantation. It wasn't just a farm, where maybe you were the only worker. You worked on the plantation and you lived in the house for free. It wasn't slavery. And I don't think it was even what they called share-cropping. That's where a man gives you a certain amount of land, you work the land, and then you get half of what you make.

Mama's husband, he got killed two months before my husband was born. His father was in a gambling game and — I never really did get an understanding of this — somehow or another, he got in a dispute about money. And this guy pulled out a gun and shot him. The shot didn't kill him right then. They brought him home and he laid there for three days before he died. The hospital was too far away. The frontier doctor came, but he couldn't get the bullet. Mama was lackin' two months of being ready to go to bed and have the baby. She used to sit on the bed beside her husband. She used to say she just knew he wasn't going to live, so she would take his hand and put it on her stomach where he could feel the baby move. And when he was conscious enough, he would talk to her concerning the baby moving in her stomach. That's when she would sit down and she would cry.

Mama married again. The way I understand it, she married again because of the two kids that she had. But she left her second husband. I asked her, "Why did you leave him?" And she said, "Well, he just wasn't the right type of person for my children. He was fine for the son I had for him. But my two older kids — he wasn't the right type for. I couldn't see living with a man that would mistreat my children. So I left him." After that, she found out that she could work. And the children, when they got big enough, used to work and help her. Then she made it just fine. She did field work, such as pickin' cotton and choppin' cotton, making gardens and things like that. And doing some domestic work.

My husband left home and went to the army. When he came out of the army, he stayed down south there with her and he farmed too, for a while. Now the oldest son, when he got out of the army, he came back to her, too. And the younger one got married. He got married rather young. I don't know at what age, but he was kind of young. Then he went into the army and he made a career out of it.

My mother-in-law never came to Chicago before she came

to live with us. She had been living in Mississippi, which I call the deep South, before she moved to Blytheville. At that particular time, her youngest son and his wife were stationed there in Blytheville. They shared a house. After that, they called my brother-in-law back to Germany and mama was there all by herself.

Mama wasn't at our wedding, because we were married here and she was there. When my husband called her and told her he was getting married and everything, she wished him all the luck in the world and asked to speak to me. We talked to each other on the phone and she said she was sorry she couldn't get here, but she was doing baby sitting work for people, and she couldn't let them down. It didn't hurt me about her not coming. She was getting old-age pension — they called it that back then — and her baby sitting work helped this old-age pension, so I didn't get upset and angry that she didn't come to the wedding. When she was in Arkansas, she shared a duplex house and she really needed that extra money — besides what my husband sent to her and what his brother sent to her. Meantime, the older son, he passed. They called it an army-related illness. Now she had been getting a check from him, too. But the government didn't give her the insurance money in a lump sum. What they did was break it up and paid it each month, so at the time she came to us, she was getting $75 a month from her older son's death, and she was getting $42 from old-age pension. She had papers to the fact that the government wouldn't decrease the amount; neither would they increase it. It would stay at $75. At that particular time, then, she really needed what she could do — the work she could get.

To put it bluntly, my husband and his mother hadn't been as close as she had been with the other kids. After he got out of the army, my husband went back to her for, I think it was, a year-and-a-half. But he didn't stay around, because he said his mother and him didn't see eye-to-eye. I didn't think it was going to be a problem or anything, having his mother live with us. If she's not paralyzed or something, I was thinking this would be a good way of having a built-in baby sitter. My children weren't a problem or anything like that. I was also thinkin', "Okay, I like fishin' and she likes fishin' too." This was a companion, someone to go fishin' with. So it was going to be a fun thing. I hadn't given any thought to it being a nuisance, or anything like that.

When mama was first here, everything was right if I did it. If my husband and I had an argument or anything like that, he was always the one that was wrong. "You should listen to your wife more often." It makes you feel good to think, "There's somebody in my corner." Nobody could say anything about me. Not even my sister. My sister would come over to the house sometimes and say, "Oh, Florence, you need to clean that stove." And mama would say, "Why don't *you* clean it? Flo's busy around here all day long. She don't have time to clean the stove like it should be cleaned. You're not doing anything, why don't you clean it for her?" It was kind of funny sometimes, the way she would be. She was a sweet person — then. I realize now that she was always that way — you know, sweet. It was her sickness that made her the way she was later on.

One morning I went into her room and asked her how she was. And she said, "I don't feel good this morning, I don't think I can get up." And I said, "Oh yeah, you can get up." But when I got behind her and kinda raised her shoulders, she screamed, and I said, "What's the matter? Is the arthritis hurtin' that bad?" She said, "Pretty bad."

Now we lived on the third floor, and I couldn't get her down the steps to take her to the doctor. My husband was at work, so what was I going to do? I got the telephone book, and started looking for doctors. It doesn't say in the telephone book that this or that doctor makes house calls. So I was just calling a variety of doctors, asking them if they would come out. We didn't have a family doctor. So I called this particular doctor, and I said, "Do you make house calls?" And he said, "No, no I don't. What's your problem?" I said, "My mother-in-law has arthritis and she's in tremendous pain." The doctor asked where I live. "I'm afraid to make house calls," he said, "because I'm afraid of being stuck up. People think I've got dope in my bag. If I come into your building, could you meet me downstairs?" I said, "Sure." When the doctor came, I took a gun downstairs along with me — just in case. (We had a pistol in the house.)

So the doctor came, and he looked at her. He told her, "You have arthritis pretty bad. How long have you had it?" She told him forty years. He asked, "What has anybody been doing for it?" Mama says, "My doctor said there's nothing they can do for it." So this doctor gave her two shots, and the next morning, she was completely paralyzed from the waist down, and her feet and her knees were swollen out of all proportion. She had been with us about four months then. She had to use the bedpan and, at that particular time, she weighed 142 pounds. Like I said, my husband was working, so there was no one but me to lift her onto the bedpan and all. But we managed.

I would get up every morning and fix the kids their breakfast. Then I would put them in her room with their toys, so they could play and I could tend to her. I would clean her up and then I'd fix her breakfast. Now she could feed herself, but her hands would shake so bad that half the food would be spilled. And I'd say, "You're not getting any benefit from this, so I'll just feed you. Is it okay if I feed you?" Well, at that particular time, she didn't want to be fed. She wanted to do it herself. And I just had to let her do it, and if she spilled it all, I just got some more.

This went on for six months. Then she got to where she could kinda raise up and move her legs. All of a sudden, she got to where she could use a walker. And she began to walk on the walker. She'd get around real good. But one particular night, when she was on the walker, she fell. She fell against the iron radiator and knocked a big gash in her head. We rushed her to the hospital, and they sewed her head up and they kept her over night. She was all right the next day.

Mama was doing fine for a while, there. She got where she could go anywhere she wanted to in the house. When he wasn't working, my husband and I would take her downstairs — me on one side him on the other — so she could take some exercise and walk outside with her walker. We'd go to the store and places like that. Or we'd go to the park. She'd even walk from the house to Jackson Park, which was a little more than a half-block. She'd walk there and she'd walk back. Of course, she'd be stopping along the way.

Mama was sick off and on from about 1972 to 1978. And it was during that time that my husband got arthritis. When he was first taken down with it, it was just a matter of hurtin'. So they told him to stay off work for a while. Well, he couldn't lift anything and if he'd bend over, he couldn't straighten back up. My husband would get up in the morning, and he couldn't put his shoes on — not just because he couldn't bend over, but because his feet would be so huge, swollen so bad. Every move was a constant ache. Then they're telling him, "You can't work any more. We want you to stay off your feet." And here, he had a family to take care of. Every job he goes for, they look at him and say, "Well, you can't pass the physical." Or the doctor would call him in and tell him, "Okay, I can pass you. All I've got to do is put down, 'okay,' but you're not going to make it. You see, what the company don't want is you to go in and maybe you can give them only six months or maybe a year. The company can't afford that. So why don't you take your doctor's advice and stop work?" But how do you tell a man to stop working when he's got a family?

Up until this time, I was working three days a week. When mama first came, I could leave the children with her. There was a lady friend of ours who lived right next door and she would come over and see after my mother-in-law and my children. Then she would work the other two days and I would do the same thing by her children. So that's how I got to work, and I kept working like that up until we moved.

We finally moved to a first-floor apartment, and I thought that things would be better for her. I could get her outside by myself. She was losing weight and, at that time, she weighed 113 or 114 pounds. So I could easily get her out in the yard. I put a chair out in front where she could sun herself. I thought everything would be better. And maybe it would have, but she was gettin' — I don't know whether you would call it senile — a lot of people say contrary. She wanted her way all of the time. I guess she really was senile, because you could sit down and talk to her and she would start talking about things that she had already told you about her childhood and so forth. And she couldn't remember. You could fix her breakfast, give her her breakfast, feed her her breakfast, and 10 or 15 minutes later, she would say, "When are you going to feed me breakfast?"

Mama had a lot of mouth, and she liked to talk. But about 1978, she had quieted down, and you could tell she was gettin' worse. Her elbows, where they had been straight, were just knots and they were crooked. She had to give up the walker, because she didn't have strength enough to lift it. All she wanted to do was sit and read the Bible. Her eyesight was tremendous. She could read the Bible without her glasses. And she loved to work those search word puzzles, where you search and find the word and then you mark it down. She'd work those and read the Bible. All she lived for then was for her youngest son to come home from Germany. She was going to go live with him.

I always felt that mama preferred her youngest son and his wife to my husband and me. They would send her a Christmas box — you know, gifts — and she would get a telephone call from them on Christmas. She'd also get a letter from them about every two months. But the whole time she was with us, she only got one Mother's Day card. Hearing from them would be what she would look forward to. Whenever she would sit up and talk, it was always about them. And I guess you could say I felt that she was putting them up to be too much. Why did she think they were so much better than us? Okay, maybe he has made a career out of the army, maybe he does have a brand new car, maybe he can afford to send his daughter, Janice, to college. But this is when I get resentful, because I'm doing something and they're not. They don't even call and want to know how she's really doing. Yet they are everything. As I said, whenever she would sit up and talk, she'd say, "Janice doesn't do this or she didn't do that." Usually this was a comparison with my daughter. Also, mama would say, "Do you know that Janice was born in Germany? Janice is a German." And I'd say, "Yes, but you and I know what she really is."

My husband and his mother used to argue. Sometimes she would say, "If I was with R. J., so and so, and so and so would happen." R. J. is what they called my husband's brother. And my husband would say, "Well, mama, I'm doing all I can." He'd say, "I didn't make a career out of the army, and maybe I should have, but I didn't. And I have a wife and family, too. And the job I had was not the type of job that paid me enough to go on a California vacation every year or go to New York. But I'm doing what I can." And he'd say, "If you don't appreciate that mama, there's nothing I can do about it."

My husband felt as though his mother didn't care anything about him, that she favored the other children more than she did him. As he put it, he was the black sheep. He used to sit down and cry and say so many things happened when he was a teenager that his mother didn't love him. And I'd tell him, "No, I think she loves you. She went through so many different situations. Your father died before you were born, then she had another husband that wasn't good to you all. It just so happened you wasn't old enough, I guess, to understand the things she had to do or the things she did do.

At one time, I believed my husband didn't love me, because he wanted me to do all these things and because he wouldn't talk to his brother. I resented him because he wouldn't talk to his brother. I figured he could've talked to his brother and told him, "You've got a wife, I've got a wife, let's make a deal. You send your wife here and give my wife a week's vacation. She's not asking for three weeks or three or four months."

Instead, my husband would say, "Yes, I love you. You know, when we first started out, we started out pretty rough, but we both believed the old saying that whatever happens, we're going to make it." "I believe," he said, "that we can make it." He said, "I trust mama with you and I don't trust her with R. J.'s wife. I know you're not going to hurt mama, you're not going to do anything intentionally to hurt her." Then he would say, "Flo, you'll survive. Mama's not going to make it."

Then mama got sick. Well, she was always sick, but she began to get sicker. And as she would get sicker, she would want me around her more. You know, she would want more of my time. Now my husband's arthritis was bad then, and he would want a lot of my time, too. It was just like I was a yo-yo. I was being pulled from one to the other. Of course, now, it became a matter of where my husband couldn't do anything for mama. So I had to decrease my work. In the morning before I would leave, I would give my husband his breakfast and my mother-in-law her breakfast, and then they could do pretty well until I got home. We had good friends — ladies that didn't go to work — and they would stop in during the day. I could still manage to get in at least one or two days' work a week.

Do you know when my situation really began to get to me? It was when my brother-in-law and his family got a leave. Mama had been with us about seven years by then. They stopped by the house before they went to Washington. While they were here, he and his wife and I were sittin' on the porch talkin'. (My husband was in the back.) And my brother-in-law says, "I'm so glad that mama is here with you all." He says,

"This is where she needs to be — with her older son. You see, they are so much alike." Then, he says, "There's another thing. My wife likes to go. She'll get in her car," he says, "and she'll be gone from morning til night." And, he says, "I can't see myself stopping my wife from doing the things she wants to do. I can't see myself making my wife take care of mother. That's not her job." I began to see then how he really felt about mama. This is her youngest son talking. And here's me, I'm the daughter-in-law. "It's okay for you to do it, but my wife's not going to do it. I'm not going to tie my wife down to this." But this all passed over, and I didn't think about it any more. Maybe I blocked it out or something.

It came back to me after we moved — about two years later. My brother-in-law and his family had been in Germany and then they came back to the states. They were living in Washington. So R. J. called mama on the telephone. "Mama, do you want to come to Washington?" "Yes." "Okay, when we go on our vacation, I'm gonna come there and get you and take you back to Washington. We live in a big, roomy house, so you don't have to worry about anything. We're gonna take care of you." "When are you coming?" He set the date — July 25. On July 25, he was going to get his mother.

Well, they showed up here that evening. They had suitcases and everything with them. My brother-in-law parked, and they brought a few things into the house. I thought that was mighty strange. "Why did they bring all of that, if they were just going back to Washington?" The next morning, R. J. said, "Mama, when you see your son again, he will have made a 30-year career out of the army." She said, "What are you talking about?" He said, "I'm on my way right now to New York. I'm going back to Germany." She says, "You are?" And here, he was supposed to be coming to take her back to Washington — permanently. He had just stopped by to tell her that he was going to Germany. He never said, "I know I promised to take you to Washington." Or, "When I get out of the army, I'm still gonna take you to Washington." It was just, "When you see your son again, he'll be a 30-year career man." That was the last time she saw him. He became a 30-year man in January 1983, and she died in February.

Now this business about mama needing to be with her oldest and about R. J. not wanting to tie his wife down was really something. Here, I can't go to the store. I've got a time limit. If I go to the laundromat, I've got a time limit. I can't go anywhere. Well, I'm not the goin' type, but I mean if I was, I didn't have this freedom.

The main thing I'm concerned about in the summer is goin' fishin'. I love to fish. I can't go fishin' anymore. When I used to go fishin' by myself, my mother-in-law was so angry with me. When I came home, she didn't want me to touch her. She would be very angry with me and then I'd feel guilty that I had gone off and stayed all day. I shouldn't have gone. Fishin' is not that important. That's what I'd tell myself. And I'd even talk to myself at night, telling myself that fishin' isn't that important. "Why do you go fishin'? This's an old lady here, and why couldn't you stay at home? She needed you." Then, like I say, I'd feel guilty.

Then I would get angry at my husband. I'd think, "Why did you involve me in this?" And, "Why did I even marry you? If I'd known this, I wouldn't have married you." Now these are not things I'm tellin' him. These are things I'm talkin' to me about. And then I'd sit and I'd feel sorry for myself. But I really knew this was the only course he could take. At this particular time, we didn't know anything about nursing homes. And, of course, the first thing that comes into your mind is that there's a lot of money involved. And we didn't have that amount of money to keep her in a nursing home. The nursing homes that she could get into without much money, are the ones we had heard so much about. I didn't tell my husband how I felt, because he couldn't do anything about it, and it would just be another way of hurting him.

Then mama got really sick, just down — oh, I guess it was in April of '82. She couldn't get in the tub so you could give her a bath. She couldn't lift her leg up. During the day, I washed her up, and when my daughter came home from school, we'd give her a bath. And the next day, the same thing. Now she was getting more contrary. She wouldn't get up. She would lay there, and you could say, "Mama, get up," and she wouldn't. "Mama, get up and use the pot." And she wouldn't. "Mama, get up and use the pot." She wouldn't get up. Period. And the next thing you know, she would wet the bed or she would have a bowel movement on the bed. Later on, she *couldn't* get up. But, at this time, she *wouldn't.*

This was a problem for me. I didn't have a washing machine, and I didn't have a dryer. Now I live a block from the laundromat — that's all — but I'd have to go to the laundromat three or four times a day. I'd have to get up in the morning at six o'clock, and before I gave her breakfast, I'd have to change mama's bed, change her, and wash her up. After I do that, then, I fix her breakfast and my husband's breakfast. Now I go and take all those things that had been used overnight to the laundromat. By the time I would come home from the laundromat, I would have to change the bed all over again. The keeper of the laundromat would get so angry with me, because, the third or fourth time, I would get there about thirty minutes before he closed. And he would have to wait until I finished. It was like this every day. I would get up at six and go to bed at one-thirty or two o'clock in the morning.

One day, it really got to me. I had just cleaned her up. And I had used a lot of disinfectant and stuff to keep the house from smellin' bad. I had also disinfected the mop, cleaned everything up, and got ready to go to the laundromat. Then I walked into her room, and she had made a mess again. Well, I picked her up and I put her on a sheet on a potty chair. And she swung at me. How she got her hand up there, I don't know. But she held up her hand like she was going to hit me. I says, "What did you do that for? Don't you ever attempt to hit me. Don't ever *think* about hittin' me. Now I'm not the type of person to sit down and tell people everything I've done. But the things I have done for you! Don't you ever raise your hand at me. I don't know what I might do. The minute you put your hands on me, I may go crazy. So don't do that. I've done things for you that your mother never did for you. So don't attempt to put your hands on me. If you can't say, 'Flo, get outta here.' Or, if you can't — every once in a while — lay your hand on me in a caressin' way, then don't touch me! Don't touch me!"

My husband came into the room, and I said, "Don't you put your hands on me either!" By now, I'm in a state where I don't know what I'm doin', where I'm goin', or where I've been. Doesn't anybody care what I'm going' through? Afterwards, after it was all clear, I went in there and changed her. When I was ready to leave the room, she kept lookin' at me. She was really talkin' to me with her eyes. So I sat down on a chair and I just sat there for a while. I think, she was sayin' "I'm sorry. If I did anything, I'm sorry." But it was just gettin' to me. Then I kept asking myself if I had been too rough on her. Was I being too rough in being agitated over the fact that she did it all over again?

I shouldn't have whooped and hollered. Why couldn't I have picked a time when she was in her right mind to let off steam? I wanted her to *know* what I was saying. I wanted her to know what I was going through. But she didn't realize it. She didn't understand it. It probably didn't get through to her.

At this time, I was going back and forth to the doctor, because my hair was coming out and I had lost all of my eyebrows. And I was losing weight. Have you ever heard of anyone losing weight like this? I would go to the doctor one day, and maybe I weighed 210. The next day, I would weigh 205. Then it would be 198 and then down to 194. And the doctor couldn't find out what was wrong with me. But the weight was just falling off me. I lost more than 40 pounds. My hair was gone, so I had to wear a wig. My eyebrows were gone, so if I wanted to go anywhere and look any way decent, I had to use eyebrow pencil. I was just naked of hair.

Finally, this one doctor did say, "What's happening? You have a problem." So I began to tell him. "My god," he said, "you're a bundle of nerves! It's stress, and you've got to find some time for yourself." He said, "Just forget everything for at least an hour each day." Now how can you forget an 85-year-old woman laying in the bed calling, "Flo, come here. Flo. Flo"? How can you forget that? How can you hear it and not go see what's wrong. Of course, there's never anything wrong, but how can you just sit and say, "I'm gonna ignore you?"

I used to be so tired, and I would hear her call and I would get up to go, and then I'd sit back down. "I'm not goin' now. I'll just wait a few minutes. But what if she's in a situation where she'll hurt herself? So then, I'd get up and go. Sometimes, my husband would hold me in bed, and he's say, "Mama don't want anything. When you go in there, she won't say a word. You'll ask her what she wants. Nine times out of ten, if she's wet, you're gonna know that anyway, 'cause you check on her every ten or fifteen minutes. So don't go." "How can I lay here and not go? There's an old person laying in there. It's like a child — a baby. How can you hear a baby crying in the kitchen and sit there and not go to see what's wrong? I have to go." It's killing me to get up and go, but I have to go. Anyway, it feels peaceful when I do come back and sit down. At least I knew I went that time.

Not long before mama died, my husband had to go to the hospital. The doctor told him he wanted him in the hospital for about three weeks. My husband said, "How can I go to the hospital?" I said, "It's okay, we can handle it." I'm the type that believes that whatever there is coming, you can handle it if you just try hard enough. "You go to the hospital. I don't want you down." So he went to the hospital. He was gone a week, and mama was getting worse and worse and worse. I had to call my husband and tell him I had called the doctor for mama. He said, "I'll be home in an hour." Just as he got home, the doctor was gettin' ready to leave. And the doctor told him, "Your mother's dying. I don't know when. It might be tonight, it might be two or three days," he said, "but she's dying. The best thing for you to do is put her in a home. Take her to the hospital, then put her in a home."

We took mama to the hospital and she laid there for three days. Then they transferred her to a nursing home. In the meantime, we had called her other son and told him to come home, that mama was very sick. But he didn't come then. I guess he didn't believe us about how sick she was, because he called his brother-in-law, who was a minister here, and told him to go to the hospital and see just how sick his mother was, then report back to him. His brother-in-law did this and he reported back that she was layin' up there in bed, lookin' like a doll. And she was fine. She even knew him when he walked in.

We called my brother-in-law three days later, when mama went to the nursing home. "I'll be there Saturday." Saturday is four days later. She died before that. We called him again. "I'll be there. I'll be there." He came, but he said his situation wouldn't let him come before she passed. What he was really telling us was that he was financially unable to come at that particular time. Now you'd think that a man who has spent 30 years in the army would have some way of borrowing the money.

I called R. J. on the night that mama died — well the morning she died. I said, "Mama's dead." Then I said, "What about mama's insurance. All she had was a $200 burial policy. What about the insurance you had on her? If you have the address, get in touch with the insurance company." "We don't have any insurance on her." "She said you did." "Oh, we let that insurance drop when she left the state." "Well, why didn't you tell somebody? She didn't know you dropped it." Then R. J. turned and said, "Min, why didn't you tell Mama?" Min got on the telephone and told me that the insurance wasn't good outside of Arkansas. Now I don't know of any insurance like that.

"Don't worry about the insurance," R. J. says, "I'll handle everything from this end." So R. J. called the W. Culberson Funeral Home and told them what he wanted. The man told him how much it would be and then R. J. calls my husband back and tells him to go down and look at the coffin. My husband and I go down there and look at it. You know how a coffin looks. Well this one was peeling — the outside was coming off. You could see the steel or whatever it's made out of. Well, we didn't want that. We know she's going in the ground and everything, but we don't want that.

So my husband says, "Did R. J. send the money?" "Oh, yes." "Well, with the money he sent, how much do we have to add to get something better?" The man told him and my husband said, "We'll pay it." What little money that my husband and I had, we were gonna use it for mama's funeral. That, plus the $200 from the burial policy, which wasn't $200 at all. It was just $160. We paid $604. Now R. J. hadn't said anything about flowers. So we went out and got $300 worth of flowers — flowers for the whole family. I had to laugh about all of this. It was so funny. In my mother-in-law's eyesight, we weren't important. We were just people to take care of her until her other son came home from the army. That's the reason she was there with us. As it turned out, my husband's big shot brother had to borrow $20 to go home. That was funny. Of course, he's never mentioned that. And neither have we. But that's okay.

I hope nobody has to go through with me, what I went through with mama. I've told my son and daughter, "Look, if I get really down, if I can't go to the bathroom, or if I can't fix my food, and if you're afraid to leave me in the house by myself, then put me in a nursing home. Somebody will take care of me if you're not able. It may not be exactly what you want, but they'll take care of me." And then my kids say, "Mama, don't talk like that!"

But why should I tie them down? I have had a reasonably good life, so don't make yourself feel sorry for me. Just put me in a home somewhere, because I know what taking care of me will do to you. If you tried to treat a sick person the way you would want to be treated if you were sick, and do all the things that have to be done for them, you'd be killin' yourself. You'd be takin' something away from your own self. And I don't believe that's fair. Life is short. And it's not fair. I have a husband, I got kids. I've lived the kind of life I wanted to live. I had fun. I went to parties, I went to dances, I went to church, and I went to quilting bees. Here this young person, my kid, comes along. And he gets to the age of 26 or 27, and he's tied down with a sick mother or a sick father. What about his life? He hasn't had all the things I have had. And if he's 40 or 50, he probably won't be physically able to do it, and his nerves won't be up to it.

I don't think it's fair for me to put these things on my children — not if they can put me in a home somewhere. Come to see me? Yes, every once in a while. At first, it wasn't my choice to put my mother-in-law in a home. When she first began to get sick, this subject came up. But I didn't see that she was in shape where she should be in a home. She could go to the bathroom. She could clean herself. And she could half way feed herself. But at the point where she needed a nursing home, nobody wanted her put in a home. Nobody but me. We didn't put her in a home until the doctor told us to.

We had discussed it as a possibility, but that was when every time you picked up a paper you'd read that some nursing home did this or did that — whippin' the old people, not treatin' them right, not cleaning up after them, lettin' them lay in urine for days. I could see no way of putting my mother-in-law in a place like that. It was like I wanted her in one, but I didn't want her in one. I guess if I could have had it just like I wanted it then, yes, I would have wanted to put her in a home. But I wasn't sure then.

I think I could take being in a home, because I don't want

my children to have to suffer through this. I don't want them to miss out on anything because of me. I wouldn't want my daughter to say, "I didn't go to college because of mama." "I didn't marry because of mama. I had to tend to mama, and there wasn't any husband that was going to stand for that." I don't want that. Cause mama has lived her life. To me, that's just like eatin' up all the ice cream from the baby. You've got a small amount of ice cream in the fridge. And here's the baby wantin' ice cream and you're wantin' ice cream. So you give the ice cream to the baby. Now a lot of people would say, "Oh, my god, the baby's got years and years to eat ice cream. And you don't have that many." But how many years have I been eating ice cream? Let the baby have the ice cream.

My husband and my children, they know how I feel about this. I tell them all the time, but they don't want to talk to me about it. And my husband won't talk about the subject.

What kind of advice would I give someone in my place? I really don't know, because you do things for different reasons. I had a reason for what I did. My reason was that I love my husband and this was his mother. He wanted his mother with us. So that was my reason. I can't really give any advice, except I would suggest not doing it, if there's any way of getting out of it. It takes away a part of your life. Just like a penitentiary would if you were behind bars. It takes something away. Something that you miss.

Many a day, my daughter would walk through the house and say, "Mama, why can't we have mother and daughter talks?" Well, by the time we would sit down and start, I would have to go and wash or somebody would call or my son would come in. I would always try to have food ready for my son — a sandwich or something on the table — when he walked in the door from school. To me, this was part of my motherhood. For him, this was part of his childhood — remembering that his mama used to have food ready for him when he came home from school.

One time when my husband was working, he had a job that paid $85 a week. I think he brought fifty some dollars home. Now I would to the store and get food, and I would get steak, but I would get round steak and it was *tough*. I'd put this steak in the oven and broil it with mustard or steak sauce on it. Then I'd call my son, who was downstairs playing, and I'd give him a piece. Even today, he'll tell me, "Mama, do you know what I remember most about when I was six or seven or eight years old? You callin' me up to eat that tough steak." Then he'll say, "Mother, why don't you buy some more?"

Those are the things that I have missed. That's what I'm talking about. I've missed sittin' down and discussin' things with my daughter — things that she wanted to talk about. Her boyfriends, something she liked, or some girl she didn't like. I never had the opportunity. I never had the chance. I didn't want to miss out on anything about my children growing up. In fact, I'd tell my kids when they took pictures, "All those pictures belong to me." "Mother, you want *all* of the pictures?" "Yes, because one of these days, you're gonna be older, you're gonna be married, and you're gonna be gone. And all your father and I will be left with is the pictures and our memories.

I want my kids to have memories, too. Doing what I did takes away from your family. It takes something away from your husband. After a while, he says, "You don't have time for me any more." He doesn't know how precious time is, because when you're not doing anything, it's because you're so tired, you can't.

Like I said, the only advice I can give is to get out of it if you can. Find a nice nursing home. Everybody's not cruel. Make sure you go visit them. Make 'em feel wanted — if they're in their right minds — by going to visit. That, I think, is the best for you and for them, too.

I think my relationship with my husband may be better because of what we went through. Now, a lot of times, he'll say, "I love you." If gratitude is the only reason, then that is not acceptable. But he'll tell me, "I try to picture my life without you, and I don't see one." I'm grateful, I appreciate that, and I love that. Maybe that's his way of asking, "What would have happened if you hadn't been in the picture for me and for my mother?"

At one time, it was an experience for me to have mama here and to wait on her. I didn't mind it. But then I got to resent it. When I did resent it, I would look back and think what a nice person she was when she was in her right mind, and that would make it a little easier. She was a very nice person. I think that it was in the last seven or eight months of her life that I would ask, "Where is this all going? Is no one going to come forward and say, 'Isn't there something I can do for you?'"

One Christmas, my brother-in-law and his family sent mama $50, and they sent my son and daughter each $50. Somebody told me that I should have resented that. "They should have sent you $50." I said, "No, I don't want $50." I would have appreciated them giving me two or three days — or even one day — off to go fishin'. I didn't want their money.

IT STILL STIRS UP MEMORIES

Pat Hughes and her brother managed their mother's care from a distance, visiting as frequently as possible. While the situation affected them both emotionally, it was the hardest on Pat. For her, the experience stirred up unhappy memories of her childhood — memories that bother Pat to this day, more than five years after her mother's death.

We lived in a large house when I was growing up — one that had been built for my grandfather. Mother had lived in it for most of her life from the time she was eight — with the exception of the first years of her marriage. After my grandparents died, my uncle and some of his friends lived in the house for several years. But, in 1929, my father bought out my mother's brothers and sisters — without telling my mother — just because he wanted it. The house is a big, beautiful old place — one with 14 rooms.

After my father died, in 1958, my mother stayed on in the family home. But she always had a student or someone staying there with her. The first student she had was a perfectly delightful young anthropologist. He was an Englishman and she was an Anglophile. So, of course, it was impossible — ever — to get someone that good again. Mother would usually have a couple of students — graduate students — but she'd have older people as well. For years, there was a high school teacher who took care of the furnace and things like that. He was the one who referred to mother as "The Queen." (Mother was very much the Grande Dame and, to me, very domineering.) Now the teacher was the fair-haired boy. He could do no wrong.

There was one story I got about my mother from my grade school principal — a woman I was always afraid of. One time when I visited the school, as an adult, the principal and I were talking about the fact that I stuttered very badly when I was in school. I said it was probably because my mother was so domineering. Then the principal volunteered that she had been scared to death of my mother. I was astonished, but I'm sure my mother sailed into her office one day and quietly raised hell.

Although mother could be a really delightful person, my relationship with her was very bad. It was a good relationship intellectually, but a bad relationship emotionally. That is, I could sit and play Scrabble with her and enjoy it, but I simply couldn't handle emotional situations.

My father hadn't been able to handle emotional situations either. Mother and father were married during the first world war and mother immediately became pregnant. My father went off to France before the baby was born. Apparently, my mother's doctor, a friend of the family, hadn't measured her pelvis properly, so after three days of labor, they had to crush the baby's skull so mother could deliver. Meanwhile, my father had gone to the front, believing she was dying. When he came back, they simply didn't discuss the baby. They never discussed it during the next 35 years of their marriage. In the same way, emotional things were never discussed in our family. Anything that was emotional was always put aside. I didn't know of the baby until I was 12, when mother let the information slip. It was another 15 years before she and I talked about it. I don't remember my father ever mentioning the baby.

I guess there had always been a problem of communication — certainly there was in my father's family. For instance, I've heard that when my uncle and aunt had guests, my uncle would visit for a few minutes and then he would retire to his study and have a drink. And that was the end of his sociability. My father's sister was a little strange, too. She was an excellent kindergarten teacher, and she had a bubbly personality. But emotionally, she couldn't deal with things. For years, I would call my aunt whenever I was in the East, but she always had a cold, and wouldn't let me come to see her. If any of the family knocked on the door she wouldn't let them in. Instead, she would suggest that they meet in a nearby restaurant.

My mother's mother was a very strong-willed woman who was highly respected in the community. Mother's father was blinded in an accident when he was a young professor. Everyone adored my grandfather, who died when I was only two years old. My mother was very close to him. So much so, that I don't think she ever got over his death. There was one episode that I remember very clearly. Some months after father's death, mother was sitting at the kitchen table crying. Now I had heard her cry only twice in my life before my father's death. I assumed her crying had something to do with his death. As it turned out, though, she was crying because she missed her own father. I reached out and took her hand. I finally let go, because I might as well have been holding a dead fish. She was too wrapped up in her own grief to notice me.

Later on, I was visiting mother when she was fairly senile. She got up in the middle of the night and wanted to know why her parents weren't in their rooms. After all, this was the house she had grown up in. I sat down and tried to tell her that if her mother and father were alive they would be over 100 years old. She couldn't believe that. They were supposed to be in their rooms. Then mother got up and said "I have to find someone who will tell me the truth."

Mother was never what I would call a very trusting person. And, as she got older she got paranoid. This was the thing I found most difficult to deal with. Things would "disappear," and when I was home, visiting, I would spend a great deal of time looking for them. At one time, I had taken a lot of pictures of the furnishings in the house for insurance purposes. She would look at these pictures and say, "See those two mirrors? They've disappeared." I would go into the upstairs hall and they would be hanging exactly where they were in the photograph.

After mother had a cataract operation, she claimed that

things had disappeared while she was in the hospital. Of course, that made me feel guilty for not having stayed in the house while she was in the hospital. Instead, I had come when she was ready to leave it, so I could take her home.

There was a time when I was looking for a whole list of things, including two pieces of fabric. When I went and produced one of them, she put it aside. Her only interest was in the one I couldn't find. I finally decided that this whole exercise was a dead end, because I wasn't giving her any pleasure by finding things. She was always interested only in what I couldn't find. My greatest help in this came from my therapist, who explained that, to mother, possessions equaled powers — that is, "I'm not losing my powers, someone is stealing my possessions." No wonder I couldn't please her by finding things.

There were other incidents that showed her paranoia. One time, mother decided that one of the roomers was dangerous, so she locked herself in her room for three days to protect herself from this nice freshman girl. I later found a stash of food hidden in her room. Another incident involved another roomer — a man of about 40, who was a history buff, and who had lived in the house for years. He was a perfectly nice guy, but not really very social. At one point, my mother couldn't find a magazine that carried a piece that she had written about my great uncle. And mother was absolutely convinced that the roomer must have stolen it. So she said to me that if she ever found out he had really stolen it, she was going to kill him. Well, as it turned out, we found several copies of the magazine when we cleared the house out some time later. Mother was always misplacing things and blaming someone else.

Sometimes mother would suddenly decide that someone living in the house had taken something. And then that person would have to go. One time, she was throwing out a coed. And it happened that the girl's father was there. He was fit to be tied and he insisted that my brother write a letter — a sort of letter of recommendation. The girl's family just couldn't believe that mother wasn't going to go around bad-mouthing this girl. This happened during the period that mother was still able to get out and around.

Mother was always worried that someone was going to steal her flat silver. One day, she came downstairs and the silver was not in the silver drawer. "It's gone! It's been stolen!" Then there was a flurry of telephone calls. As far as I could make out later, mother had transferred the silver from the drawer to the locked liquor cabinet. She subsequently transferred it to her own — by then locked — bedroom closet. Anyway, mother accused one of the aides of stealing the silver, so, of course, the girl had to be reassigned.

Sometime later, when my brother and I were visiting mother, we had found all of the silver and gotten it out of the closet. It wasn't just the flat silver by that time. Mother had put a lot of the other silver in the closet, too. She was in bed at the time, so we spread all of the stuff out on the bed. Mother looked at some of the pieces of silver and said, "Well, you know, that's the silver Iris stole." My brother said, "Then how come it's here now?" Mother said, "They made her give it back." Mother just couldn't be wrong. She had the most convoluted ways of being right. No way would she ever have admitted that the silver hadn't been stolen, when she had insisted that it had been. There were many similar episodes. And mother was extremely clever about getting out of ever being wrong about anything.

I remember, for example, the one exception happened when I was living out in California with a roommate. My roommate and I sang in the church choir, and every week after rehearsal, we'd go to someone's house for cocoa and cookies. Mother visited during that period, and when it was our turn to entertain, after rehearsal, nothing would do but that we have punch and this and that. We had to make a big deal out of it, which was totally inappropriate and embarrassed me considerably. But I couldn't stop it. Some time later, she did admit she was wrong.

My first inkling of mother's senility came after my brother

and I visited her the same weekend. He and his family arrived Friday morning and I arrived Friday evening. Then I left on Sunday, several hours before my brother and his family left. Mother called me two days after the visit and said that she had had such a nice visit with the family and that they had all missed me. I was absolutely stunned! I didn't have the wit to say, "Look, I was there most of the time they were." Now, I was devastated, because I didn't know what was happening. You know, it was an effort to get there and, of course, I got the feeling that the effort went down the drain.

Mother would also lay another guilt trip on me. When I had been there and when she remembered I had been there, she would call and tell me how much she wanted me to come again. It was as if she thought I should be spending every weekend there. No matter how often I went, it wasn't often enough. It was very difficult for me. That's why it was essential for me to go to a therapist. I would have gone berserk with this pressure. I don't think she did the same thing to my brother. It was a very curious thing — this calling me. She would call when I hadn't been there and say, "Well, you were here last night. Why did you leave without saying anything?" My brother never got this treatment.

It finally became necessary to have someone come in, on a regular basis, to take care of mother. After we talked mother into the idea, we contacted Home Care, Inc., a local home health agency. In the beginning, someone came in twice a week. Then it was every day, then every day and every evening, until finally there was an aide or a practical nurse in the house all the time. What we didn't know when we made the arrangement with HCI was what came with it. There was a fabulous field nurse — a part of the service — who would come every month, or every day, depending on what was needed. The field nurse was a godsend. She was someone that mother could call when she had a problem.

Shortly after we made these arrangements, the practical

nurse came in and found that mother had fallen in the bathroom and couldn't get up. Mother fell on other occasions, too. One of the times was when I was there. I was sleeping in the bedroom next to hers. And, in the middle of one night, I heard a thud. So I got up and went into the hall. Mother had wandered out of her room and fallen. She hadn't hurt herself, because she was really well padded. I got her onto a throw rug and pulled her over to the top of the steps, because she kept saying that she could get up if she could hold onto the stair railing. I got her back up. Then I got her back into her room. It was pretty hairy. This happened during the time that the aides were not there overnight.

About this business of falling, the field nurse — who was a perfectly marvelous person — said one day, "You know, we think part of her problem of falling is that she has taken to eating one TV dinner a day and lots of sherry and cookies." Mother used to tell me that TV dinners were marvelous because they gave her a balanced diet. At that stage, she was so certain of her ability to run things that she was becoming malnourished. But, of course, I couldn't get her to do anything about it. Finally, the aides were preparing meals and seeing that she ate decently. I don't recall her falling after that.

During the time mother was being cared for by the aides, she would call up very upset and she'd tell me I would have to do something about them. Mother would read in the day book kept by the aides that someone had been in to give her a massage, but mother said the girl hadn't done it. Well, my guess is that mother probably had forgotten she had had the massage, so she said that she hadn't had it. Of course mother decided the girl was lying — that she was saying she had done something that she really hadn't.

Also during this period of time, I'd get many early morning phone calls from one of the HCI people because when they came, mother would tell them how I had been there and then had simply left without telling anyone where I was going.

Mother could not understand why, when the nurse called, I was in Philadelphia when I should have been in Providence.

This whole thing was part of her paranoia. Even so, it was hard to take. It was difficult for me, because there was an unfairness about it. And it was much too reminiscent of her unfairness to me when I was young. I always thought I got the short end of a lot of things that I would never be allowed to do. This was because I was younger and because I was a girl. A good deal of emphasis was placed on the fact that I was a girl. I don't think that I ever blamed my brother because I felt I got the short end of things.

I remember, when I was 12, being very pleased with myself because I had ridden my bike to the next town and back. But I caught hell for that because it was dangerous. Now if my brother had done that at age 12, it would have been all right. I think my mother and father were absolutely convinced that I was going to get raped. They were much more concerned about things like that than my friends' families were. And I was completely brainwashed by it.

I remember other things from my childhood. I had had asthma as a kid and was in and out of the hospital a lot. Now, physical pain was acceptable in our family, but not emotional pain. I remember mother being very sympathetic when I was crying because of cramps, but crying because I was unhappy wasn't tolerated. Once I hid in my closet to cry, and father made me come out and stop crying. I think the worst part of my relationship with my parents was when I was an adolescent. (They didn't have the slightest idea about depression.) Often when I was unhappy, I would disappear for hours. Somehow or other, my disappearing upset them. Even so, I wasn't willing to discuss it.

Mother was concerned that I didn't date, but then she didn't like the boys I knew. They weren't "top drawer." And the girls at camp weren't top drawer either. They didn't have the right accent, and mother was very conscious of that. I got along. They were okay kids, even if my mother didn't approve of them. As a matter of fact, there are very few people I can think of that I knew through grade school and high school who were totally accepted by my parents — unless, of course, they were children of people we knew.

A great deal of the pressure that was put on me, I think, was the result of the death of mother's first child. Had the baby lived, she would not have had me. Mother had wanted to have two children, and the first one died. She had trouble carrying the second child — my brother — and she had to talk her doctors into letting her carry me. So you see, I was the substitute for the dead boy.

Adolescence was pretty terrible for me. And the situation with my mother stirred all of this up to a point where I dreamed about it. I dreamed one night that I saw one of the HCI girls walking out of mother's house. When my mother started making remarks about this girl, I dreamed that I put my hands around my mother's neck and said, "If you ever do that again, I will surely choke you!" That was the kind of hostility her behavior stirred up in me. I had really had it! I didn't need that kind of behavior.

Some years ago, my therapist — misunderstanding something I had said — thought I was considering moving back to Providence and living with my mother. So the therapist said, "Well, you can commit suicide if you want to."

There came a point at which my brother and I decided that it would be nice for mother to have many visits and that we would take turns going to see her. I would go for a weekend one month and he would go for a weekend the next month. That way, she would have two visits — one with each of us — instead of one visit with both of us.

As it happened, one weekend my brother and I both planned to visit mother. That weekend, he arrived earlier than I did. I was coming by train, and he was going to pick me up at the railroad station. When I arrived, I called the house from the station. My brother answered the phone. He told me that he had given the aide the night off, and he was giving mother dinner. He said he would be right down to pick me up. I told him that I could just as easily take a cab. But he said, "No, go next door to the bar and wait for me. I want to talk to you before we go home." I said, "Okay." So I went in and sat down in the bar. A little later, my brother came in. And the first thing he said was, "I want you to know that I'm a little bit tight." Then he started telling me about the problems he was having with mother, and how she would verbally back him into a corner — you know, questions similar to the classic, "Yes or no. Have you stopped beating your wife?" And he was going batty with it. It was an absolute revelation to him when I said, "Yes, she does that to me, too."

Right at this point, it became clear to us that we would visit her together in the future. Neither one of us could cope with it alone. From then on — oh, every two or three months — we would go to visit her. This was clearly a matter of self preservation. We both needed that.

Mother's senility started, probably, in the spring of 1974, but she didn't go into a nursing home until the spring of 1978. My brother and I had decided that, as long as her estate could afford it, mother would stay in her own home — that is, as long as she knew she was in her home. And, fortunately, it was possible to do this. From time to time, the field nurse would suggest a retirement home or a nursing home. Mother once allowed someone to drive her as far as the entrance of a nursing home that had just been built. When she got there, mother said, "Hmmmmmph, I'd jump out the window." She never volunteered to go into a home.

To a degree, I suppose people thought that, since I didn't have a family — and my brother did — I should be more available as a resource for mother. This never became a problem, because I don't think my brother looked at it that way. I never felt he thought that I should do more than my share because I didn't have a family. Fortunately, no one except my mother laid that on me. Her friends didn't lay it on me and neither did my brother. I probably felt that way, to some extent, but it wasn't prompted by anyone but my mother. My relationship with my brother was very positive — though it couldn't be close because of the way we were raised.

My brother was not feeling well when we visited mother in October of 1977. But he didn't know what the problem was. During our visit that month, we decided that, probably, by January, mother should be in a nursing home, because of the rate of her decline. That was one of the things that made the situation easier for me later on. I didn't have to make the decision alone, after my brother died in December. The decision had already been made. By pre-arrangement between the field nurse and me, I would not be there when mother went into the home. This was partly based on the fact that, if she had a flash of recognition at that point, it would be too difficult for me. It would make me feel very guilty, if for even a flash she knew what was happening.

As I mentioned, my brother was not feeling well that October. When he got back home to Madison, he had to have surgery. After that he lived only six weeks. He died four days before Christmas. I had gone back to see him, but had returned home, expecting to visit the family for Christmas, when my nephew called to tell me that his father was dying. A day or two later, I went back again. And I spent a lot of time with my brother the ten days before he died. Mostly, it was non-verbal time, but it was a time in which we were very, very close.

During the time my brother was so ill, my mother kept asking for him — something she had never done before, although she was always asking for me. The field nurse was the only one from HCI who knew my brother was dying. Finally, on Christmas Day, the field nurse had to tell mother that my brother had died. Mother wept for a while and then she seemed to forget it completely. That happened a year before my mother died.

When mother finally did go into the nursing home, the field nurse wrote an agreement for me that there would be no CPR used to revive mother. There would be no heroics. Mother had always been horrified that people were kept alive when they weren't really there any more and that incredible amounts of money were spent on life support systems for people who were really dead.

One morning, about a year after my brother's death, I got a phone call from the nursing home telling me that mother's blood pressure had suddenly gotten very low, and that she had been taken to the hospital. When she got to the hospital, they found she was in a diabetic coma. Now mother had never been considered a diabetic, as far as I knew. Oh, she had had some indications of diabetes, but that was all. It just suddenly happened that way. Well, they automatically pulled her out of the coma in the hospital, so that she could spend the next ten days dying of pneumonia. I felt betrayed by that. But, of course, treating someone in a diabetic coma is not considered CPR. It's not considered "extraordinary means."

My niece and my nephew spent a good deal of time with my mother when she was in the hospital that last time. One day, my nephew called me and said that mother was saying, "I love you, Mattie." Now mother had developed a habit of referring to any woman as "Mattie." We never knew who Mattie was, or where mother got this. Well, I waited a day or two before going to Providence. When I did get there, I wasn't sure whether she knew me. I had waited too long.

What I hadn't understood from the telephone call from my nephew was that my mother was saying, "I love you," and adding my name. It was a bittersweet revelation.

The family had quite a discussion with the chaplain about the time of my mother's death. We felt, and so did the chaplain, that she died before midnight on the anniversary of my brother's death. Legally, she died the next day when the hospital found her.

THERE WAS NO QUESTION. . . .
NO QUESTION AT ALL

Giving up her life in America to move to Japan was the only decision that Gigi Matsubara could make. Although she was of Japanese ancestry, Gigi was a native-born American, who had visited Japan only once. When her husband — who was considerably older than she — retired, he went to Japan to visit his homeland. It was a visit that was to become permanent. Within a year, he was terminally ill with cancer. So, for the second time in her 33-year marriage, Gigi left her home and her belongings to move to a new and alien place. There was no dilemma — only sadness — for Gigi in caring for her loved one.

I'm what one calls a second generation Japanese. I was born and raised in California, where I went through all of the problems of attending a segregated American school. Where I lived, there were more Japanese in my age bracket than in the older group, so when it came to finding a husband, we always ended up marrying somebody younger or marrying somebody who came from Japan.

My husband, who came from Japan when he was 17, was nice enough to marry me. After we were married, we started a hotel business. But then, about a half-year later, the war started, and we had to move. We left everything — my wedding presents, and everything I had gotten for my new life. Oh, what things I *could* sell, I sold, but it was very sad. We were dreading the worst when we were sent to Santa Anita. After about two months, we were sent to Heart Mountain, Wyoming.

No matter how hard we Japanese tried to be like good American citizens, other citizens would not take it that way. They would automatically say, "Oh, she's Japanese . . ." as a reminder of the war time and all of the stories of atrocities that were spread around. The rumors that went around during that time were awful. There were no facts, no truth to them. To give you an example. There was a Congressman, or something, from Colorado who splashed it all over the Denver Post that the Japanese were well fed, that they got meat every day — and that was during meat rationing. Well, he never came into our camp. You know, with Japanese cooking, you can economize. So the cook in our camp would save the meat rations and, during the week, we would be eating on very, very bare things. But, on Sunday, the cook would give us all of the meat ration, which was his way of consoling us. Maybe the Congressman heard about it, I don't know, but then he retracted what he said. Do you know where that was? Waaaaaaay inside the paper! That's why, even to this day, when I read in the paper about politicians talking this way and that way, I'm always very cynical.

California is very big, and the Japanese there were very spread around. When we went into the camp, I was amazed to see so many Japanese and so many Japanese with glasses on. In those days, I wasn't wearing glasses. Japanese mothers always thought that wearing glasses was not good. They also thought that you must have clear, clean skin. These are some of the things that Japaneses mothers always told you when you were growing up. They also told you about clean bathrooms. They always told you that when you clean the dirtiest part of the house, you will be rewarded by having a good husband.

We were in Wyoming for three and one-half years. Everyone had some kind of job to do in the camp. We all kept busy and we all worried a lot. My husband was in a plumbers' group. They kept busy fixing the plumbing, seeing that the pipes didn't freeze, and things like that. I did some work as a hairdresser. People in the camp also worked hard winterizing their barracks, because it gets awfully cold in Wyoming.

Afterwards, the government didn't want us to become

another group like the Indians — the American Indians. They didn't want us stuck on a sort of reservation, so they encouraged us — in fact they pushed us — to go out. And, of course, they paid the fare — the train fare — to wherever we wanted to relocate.

It just so happened that my oldest sister's daughter told her family to move to Chicago, so I followed my sister, and my husband and I came to Chicago. At the time, I was afraid to go back to California. They have quite a few nuts out there, you know, and I was afraid. I'm a little chicken to begin with. so I told my husband, "We'll work here for two years, and then we'll go back to California." My husband was a landscape gardener before he married me, and he thought he could do that in Chicago. But as it turned out, landscape gardening is different in Chicago because of the seasons.

Anyway, we came to Chicago and I found out — that for working — Chicago is a marvelous place. In California, I worked for a Japanese beauty salon. I apprenticed there, and they trained us to work. I mean, we worked! We didn't get much in those days, either. But I've always been grateful that I learned how to really work. It's surprising the number of people who don't know how.

When we came here, my husband had an obligation. He had to help educate many of his brothers and sisters. He was the only one they could depend on. That kind of kept us on the quiet side, because you can't splurge when you're educating brothers and sisters. We felt we should do it, though, because, my God, in Japan after the war it was a matter of where the next food was coming from. My husband was very good to his family. He saw to it that all of the children got some kind of training. The youngest wanted to become a doctor. I said, "A doctor?" "Well, if he wants to go," my husband said, "Let's do it." I said, "Okay." So we did it. I was happy to do it because my husband was so nice to me.

My husband was an unusual fella. He waited for me to

grow up, and then, I couldn't make up to him enough. My friends accused me of being very Japanese. I wasn't. I was just so grateful that my husbnad stuck by me. I was the youngest in the family, and my mother had spoiled me because I lost my father when I was very young. Oh yes, adolescence was very rough. I was very, very bratty at home, and I caused a lot of problems. But fortunately, it didn't go out of the family, because we have been told that we have to behave very good in society.

As I said, my husband was a very unusual man. I have flowers all around me, but it's not because I love flowers. It's because I have been arranging them for 30 years. I took up flower arranging because playing baseball, which I enjoyed much more, was not feminine. I thought, "Gee whiz, I had better act more like a woman." So I came home and I announced, "I'm going to take up flower arranging. The classes are at the Buddhist church." My husband looked at me, and he said, "What are you going to classes for?" I looked at him, and I said, "I'm going there to arrange flowers — to learn to arrange flowers." And he said, "Oh, no you're not." "I'm not?" "No, you're not. You're going to learn *the way of the flowers*." I'd never heard of that. I'd never heard of such a thing, so I said, "What's that?"

It's really a philosophy, I think. You learn that flowers, like people, are all individuals, and you don't try to change them unless they hurt themselves. You can't force them, because when you force an arrangement, it breaks. You also learn how different flowers look good together, because that's the way of nature. This is something I didn't know about Japanese art. Once I learned all of this I appreciated it. And it has helped me a lot. I'm very proud of the knowledge that was given to us through our culture.

After we were in Chicago for quite a while, I visited my family in California. Well, every time I go to California, I get in a big fight with my family. When I came back, my husband said, "I think we'd better stay here." And that's one of the reasons we stayed here. Another reason is that it's more relaxed here than it is in California. In California, the Japanese are working very hard to catch up. They are trying to recapture what they lost during the war. They're always working. It's quite a stressful situation. Everybody has to buy a car. And then the children have to keep up with their friends. This family does this and this family does that. Here, you can just do your own thing — practically.

Instead of being a landscape gardener, my husband went to work for a company that made ink for printing companies. He was there for 25 years, and then he retired. After he retired, he didn't know what to do. At that time, I had about one year and two months — I think — before completing 20 years with Bradberry's. And I wanted to have a record of 20 years. So I told him, "You have to wait for me. I want to make 20 years." He looked so bored that I said, "Why don't you go to Japan and see how the situation is over there. My husband had a house there — a family house — so he went to Japan, and he decided that's where he was going to retire. He also decided to remodel the house enough so that we could move in. Then we could do more remodeling after we moved in.

Deep down, I knew that he might have to take over the family responsibilities in Japan, at some point. But he was the only family I had, so I decided to go wherever he was. It was no problem to me as long as he was alive. Remember, I didn't have any family at that time, except my brother. And I didn't want to bother that poor guy with my troubles. I just accepted the situation. If my husband wanted to go to Japan, I would go, but I never dreamed it would turn out the way it did.

My husband was in Japan not quite a year when he got sick. And I think that one year is what made him sick. He was trying to remodel the house, and I found out that any kind of building project in a village like his is — what can I say? — complicated. The carpenters have to be kept fed, they have to

have their drinks, and they have to have their snacks in between. This all has to be taken care of. And then, on top of it,
he had to help them. I've never heard of such a thing. When I
found out all of this afterwards, I thought, "My God, no wonder he got sick." It was too much pressure, he wasn't used to
that. My husband always had had a bad heart. A heart spe-
cialist told me once that my husband had a small heart —
probably had rheumatic fever when he was a child. I could see,
all of a sudden, he had all of these pressures around him. I
think he would have lived longer if he hadn't had to go through
all that remodeling business. I didn't realize that life was that
complicated in Japan.

It was my husband's youngest brother — the doctor — who
told me about his illness. He told me my husband might live a
year or five years, and he said, "Why don't you quit your job
and come to Japan? Well, of course, I couldn't stay here. That
would be selfish of me when my husband was ill. My husband
was everything, after all. I couldn't put finishing 20 years at
Bradberry's before my husband. Furniture and things? That's
not important. Not having any children, my husband was all I
had. I had been with him all those years. So my husband came
back to help me break up the apartment, and I moved to Japan. I'm not as independent as I sound.

When I went to Japan, my brother-in-law gave me hope
that my husband would live longer than he did. He died a year
later. I didn't have to do much nursing while my husband was
ill, because my brother-in-law took care of that. My brother-
in-law had his own hospital in Tokyo. You see, in Japan, all
doctors who can afford it have a little hospital of their own. It's
like a clinic, but they call it a hospital. There were living quarters over the hospital, so I didn't worry too much. I felt that
any time my husband was bad, the doctors were right there.
During the time he was in my brother-in-law's hospital, I
stayed in my brother-in-law's home. It was kind of hard. I had
a language difficulty and I didn't know my way around, but I

was able to find my way on the subway to go to the Ginza and places like that.

My husband was in and out of the hospital that last year. At one point, he was transferred from my brother-in-law's hospital to a larger one, where he had surgery. In Japan, the family can stay at the hospital with the patient. There's a bed in the room. But you have to go to the public baths, because the baths at the hospital are only for patients. I stayed there with my husband for about two weeks. It was like a dream. I couldn't believe I was doing the things I was.

My husband had the kind of cancer where little tumors pop up all over, and the last tumor was in the brain. Oh, maybe it was better that way, because I noticed that his personality was beginning to change. He was deteriorating. But I never did think that he was going to die. It never dawned on me that it was going to happen — after 33 years, you know. It gets to be a habit, and it was very much of a shock to me when he did go.

When my husband was in the hospital that last time, he was so happy because all of the brothers that he had helped — the sisters, too — came to visit him. My husband died a very happy man. He knew that his brother would take care of me. And I accepted that, because I had no other choice. It was a big change for me. I had been going along at the same speed for 33 years, and then all of a sudden, all of these changes. It was really an adjustment. I didn't question anybody about anything. I just accepted it.

I was told after my husband died that this man — who saw me grow up — was very concerned about me. "She won't fit into the Japanese community." Well, I tried. I tried not to be what I read about someplace — the Ugly American. I did my darndest. I felt like telling some of these women off, but I never did. I took it. And it was hard for me. I speak Japanese — but not that well — so when they would come up and speak Japanese, I didn't always understand. They're like French people. They have phrases for certain moods and certain words for certain people. When they talked to me in the fast Japanese that they use — a dialect — I didn't understand. If we had lived in Tokyo, instead of my husband's village, it would have been wonderful. But my husband was from southern Japan, where they speak a different dialect. Even other Japanese have difficulty speaking to them — understanding them.

My husband's family owned properties, and the house was one of them. After my husband died, I was in charge of the house, and it was kind of nice to be in charge of it. I felt kind of proud of myself. I could handle it. Of course, if I really got stuck, I could always call my brother-in-law in Tokyo. But the trouble is, I couldn't get a phone. So each time, I had to go next door and borrow the phone. That was a hassle. That's why, many times, I couldn't say things to my brother-in-law that I would've if I wasn't in someone else's house. The hardest thing in Japan is to get a telephone. But, of course, I got my phone just before I left.

I think I could've taken living in Japan if my husband was alive. He had told me that when the weather was nice, we could travel. "I'll show you what Japan is like — the good and the bad. And how people live." That would have been wonderful. But when my husband died, the only place I went was to temple. You see, in this little village, where they have ancestors going back I don't know how many years, they have memorial services for all of these ancestors. Because I was in charge of the house, I had the responsibility — at certain times in the month — of going to temple for so-and-so's memorial service.

It's so much easier living in Chicago. Sure, we have Buddhist temples here, and, of course, you're supposed to go to the memorial services and all. But they don't consider it a crime or a sin if you don't go. When I was taking care of the family house — before my husband died — I had to go to temple for his two mothers, the mother that nursed him, his father, his grandfather, his brother who died in the service — that's six, and there were a few more. I tell you, in that year, I made up for all of the times I didn't go to temple in the 33 years I was married.

Being in charge of the house, I had other obligations, too. For example, there are no caterers in Japan, so when someone wants to have a dinner after a memorial service, the neighborhood people get together to prepare the meal. Now I don't know how they cook in Japan, so they would assign me to do certain things — things I had never done before. Then they would watch me to see how well I would do it. I was very embarrassed.

There was one time when the people in my district had to help pave the road or make a contribution toward getting it paved. So I spent a day moving rocks from the road so it could be paved. And I thought, "I came to Japan for this?"

Half the time I was in Japan, I wasn't too sure I was doing the right thing. And oh, I made some real big booboos. One thing about living in Japan, though, once you get the hang of it — of what's expected of you — it's simple. It's like living in the Victorian age. As long as you know what you're supposed to do — the rules — it's all right. But it was hard for me. I didn't want to blow my stack at people, because I felt that would be untrue to my American heritage. I had a lady staying with me, and you know, it's hard to live with someone else after you've lived with your husband for so long. And this woman had some unusual ways. Also, people would say things because they didn't know about America. But oh, my gosh, it was worse at election time. They tried to make me vote, because they want every vote they can get. I always said, "No, I can't vote, because if I vote, I can't go back to America."

Before my husband died, he was getting social security, which helped a lot. Although we had no rent to pay, we had water bills and electric bills and gas bills. And we had to buy food. When my husband died, like an honest citizen, I reported his death. So the checks stopped. Yet, here in the village, were people — people who never came to the United

States — getting social security checks from America. I was not 60 at the time, so I didn't get my husband's social security check. I think they've changed this now, but I was not 60 at the time my husband died, so I was not paid social security. I got no help. Instead I'm living on principal. And I'd been paying into social security since it started. And the nerve! They deny me! When I finally came back to California to visit my brother, I went to the Social Security Board to see if I could get my widow's payments again. And you know what the man told me? "You're too young." What a nice thing to say!

My flower teacher's daughter was in Japan while I was there. Her husband was with our government — U.S. Customs. After my husband died, I went to Tokyo to visit her. She said, "Why are you staying here? You don't belong here. Go back to Chicago." "But I have nothing there." "You have nothing here either." "But I have a house I'm responsible for." "Let your brother-in-law take care of that. Go back to Chicago."

I was very lonesome, and I didn't have any close friends in Japan. Also, living is harder there. It's just harder. But it dawned on me that if I came back to Chicago, I didn't have a job. I didn't know whether I could get one. I had worked for Bradberry's but that didn't mean I was going to get my job back. I also didn't know who my friends were, because I didn't need them when my husband was alive.

The day before I left my village, I had a letter from this woman who has a grocery store here — an oriental food store. She never wrote to me before. But she wrote in her letter, "If you come to Chicago, you can stay with me." I couldn't believe it. That was beautiful! I said to her after I got here, "What made you do that?" She said "Your husband," I said, "What do you mean, my husband?" Well, my husband used to go to the grocery store and buy the food for the evening, because, in my job, I worked later than my husband did. So he knew more about Edith than I did. At one time, he told her, "If anything should happen, would you be a friend to my wife?" And she had never forgotten. That's the kind of man he was. You see how he paved the way? I didn't know I had a friend. I didn't know I had a place to go. My husband had done that.

So I came back to Chicago and stayed at Edith's and went back to Bradberry's. But when I walked into Bradberry's, I realized I had a problem. You know what happened in the couple of years I was gone? Everything had gone to scissor cutting — thanks to Sassoon — and blow dry. I didn't know how to blow dry. I got my job back, but I certainly didn't want to be embarrassed. Nothing embarrasses me more than to have somebody say, "Oh, I don't like your work." I didn't have that much money, but I went to New York to the school that Bradberry's had. In those days, they had styling classes, brush-up courses, and so forth. So you see, I was forced to be on my own. It was good for me, though.

What did my husband's family think when I decided to come back? They didn't expect it. They expected me to stay there to take care of the family house, because then they can do their own thing. If I'm not there, my youngest brother-in-law has to worry about it. He was not very pleased. He wasn't pleased at all. My brother-in-law and I didn't get along too well. He was difficult to understand, because he had such a quick mind that he was always two or three jumps ahead of me. It's been ten years since I left Japan.

You learn from adversity, you do. I feel that every time you go through a hardship, you learn something from it. Like the death of my husband. I was sheltered, I was protected. I was in my little world. And when I look back, I was a very shallow person. Now, I have to be on my own, and whatever I do, I get repercussions! My husband isn't here to protect me. Naturally, I'm more aware of what I do and what I can do to other people. You learn to be more aware, and I think that makes for a better person.

I've realized more and more lately that I'm alone now. So I

had better like myself or I'm not gonna get anywhere. I was watching television — now that I'm semi-retired I have all these days off — and the program was about aging. So I thought, "Hey, maybe I had better look at this." There was one woman on the program whose husband left her after 30 years of marriage. All of a sudden, he wanted a divorce. And she talked about how she coped with it and how she went through it. At the end, the Emcee said, "Now that we're almost closing, do any of you have anything to say to the audience or to the people who're listening?" And this woman said something that I thought was beautiful. She said, "Regardless of how old I am, I try to be as lovable as I can be." And I thought to myself, "How important!" So this is what I'm trying to do with myself. I try to do things that will make me like myself. Sometimes I go to Edith's grocery store and check on her. Other times I visit my girlfriend's mothers. I poke fun at them or I tell them about some of the stupid things I've done or the mistakes I've made. I make them laugh and they love it. I make somebody happy and, in turn, I feel better. I feel like I've accomplished something.

One of my fears now is getting very old and not being able to take care of myself. I had a customer who suffered from Alzheimer's disease. She was really a very lovely person, but before my eyes, I could see her changing. She became very forgetful, she didn't cooperate, and she had to be watched. Fortunately, she had a very nice husband who brought her in and picked her up. When I realized that I couldn't control her anymore, I asked her husband to come back a little early, so he could watch her when I was doing other things or working on other custormers. Who knows? I could be like that some day.

If that should happen, I wouldn't want to depend on my friends to take care of me. Of course, I could pick up and go to Japan. I know that my brother-in-law would help me until I die. But Japan is so far away. I do worry about not being able to take care of myself, but I can't let it dominate me. My problems really aren't very great. I don't have children to worry about being cared for after I'm gone and I don't have a mother-in-law who depends on me for her care. I don't have in-laws who are hounding me to do this and do that. So, I'm really very fortunate.

I can't believe how well I'm doing right now. As I told you, I'm working part time — and it's fun. One day, one of the retired manicurists visited the salon, and she said, "Gigi, may I ask you a personal question?" and I thought, "Gee, what is she going to ask me?" "Do you have a boyfriend?" I said, "Why? Why do you ask that?" She said, "You look so happy." I told her, "It's not 'happy,' that's not the word. The word is 'relieved.'"

For some time, I had been worried about what I was going to do. Here, I'd been working all these years — past 65. "Am I kidding myself by trying to compete with these young kids?" In our business, you have to be in fashion, you have to be on the go, and you're selling yourself every day. But I thought, "If I quit, what will I do?" I was really worried. It never dawned on me that I could work part time and that it would work out so well.

Working part time, I don't have the pressure anymore. I just take care of the people who ask for me. When I'm through, and I don't have any more appointments, I can go home. Or I can browse through all of the lovely clothes in the stores.

Right now, I'm very content with my life, except for that fear — that fear of getting old and being physically or mentally incapable of taking care of myself.

THE MAGIC WORD WAS "WE"

Carol Kallish is a woman with a crusade. Seven years ago, when doctors first suspected that her mother had Alzheimer's disease, Carol went into action. She began by gathering all of the information she could find on this debilitating disease and by looking into what few resources were available to Alzheimer's patients and their families. What began as an educational necessity became a full-time commitment.

Carol and her husband, Ed, not only committed themselves to the care of Carol's mother, but they also committed themselves to the help and support of other Alzheimer's families. This is their story.

My mother was a capable, managerial type lady, who was office manager of *Television Magazine* in New York. She was married to my father, who was a career army man, for 45 years. Since father was an army man, I was raised by my mother. My grandmother lived with us, too, because my grandfather had died two weeks before my mother and father were married. My parents brought her into their home to live with them.

During my father's army career, he developed a viral-type malaria, which ended in a stroke at age 65. Mother took care of him by herself for 13 years in their home in Florida. She managed everything, asking no help from anyone. He died nine years ago, and about two years later, mother started forgetting things — like our birthdays and anniversaries. She also began repeating herself during our many telephone conversations.

From time-to-time, we went down to Florida to visit mother. During those early visits, a few things happened, but nothing that doesn't happen to all of us when we begin getting older. Mother would also come to Chicago to visit. She'd be forgetful sometimes, but we would just tease her about it, and send her back home to Florida.

Then we began to notice that this take-over, managerial woman was beginning to age. But we said, "Well, she's forgetting, but she's just getting older." At that time, mother was 67, so we just let it slide. Not too long later, we had word from relatives that things were not right. Now mother was a bookkeeper by profession, so she would be treasurer of every organization imaginable. She would also be president of organizations, and she would have many social obligations. But now this same woman, all of a sudden, couldn't balance her checkbook or remember what day it was.

When my daughter went down to Florida for college break, she went to stay at her grandmother's home. She saw how mother had been living and how she had been covering all of her little episodes. My daughter called home and said, "You'd better get down here." When we got there, we found total disarray. Mother was living on pop and cookies, and there were cockroaches throughout the apartment. Mother wouldn't let anyone into the apartment and she was fighting with everybody. She wasn't bathing.

A family relative had taken her to a general practitioner down there. Mother had a CAT scan and the doctor said that it was, possibly, Alzheimer's disease. With that, my oldest daughter called San Diego, where Andrus Gerontological Center is, to talk to her girlfriend, who is studying gerontology. My daughter said, "Send our family everything you have on Alzheimer's disease." And her friend did.

My husband and I went back to Florida, and took mother to a neurologist. The neurologist copied all of the material I had, because he didn't have any current information about Alzheimer's. This was six years ago — before Alzheimer's became THE DISEASE of the 80s. We then had a meeting with her doctor, and I said to him, "How long can she live alone?" The doctor said, "You'll know." Mother was sitting right beside us, and she never remembered being there. Right then, we made plans to bring her to Chicago. She was in the early stages of the disease when she came here. I had convinced her that she was just going to come for the holidays, and then I just never talked about her going home. That seemed to satisfy her.

When mother came here, I called the Alzheimer's Association, I also made an appointment with a doctor here in Chicago. Mother had another CAT scan — now this was 1979 — but still Alzheimer's was not the definitive word. However, the doctor did say, "Yes, I believe that the first diagnosis is right." I said, "What do I do?" He said, "Join a support group. There's nothing I can do for you." And that was it. You see, nobody knows what causes this disease or whether there is any treatment.

My husband, Ed, and I decided to keep mother in our home. We did it, partly, because we realized that she was on a pension from the government, which in no way would cover institutionalization. And even though she wasn't anywhere near needing institutionalization, we couldn't send her back to Florida without getting steady help for her — someone to be with her. There was really no discussion about that. Being an only child helped in that particular situation, because my husband and I could make all of the decisions. Ed and I decided that this is what we would do, because that's the way we were raised.

From early on, my housekeeper, who had been with me for 20 years, decided she wanted to help. She is a good and kind woman, and my mother had known her all those years. When my housekeeper told me she wanted to help care for my mother, I said, "Can I put a white uniform on you and will you be her nurse and friend? You won't have to do too much, just be her friend." And so mother and my housekeeper had, for over a year, a unique relationship. They went shopping. They went to lunch. They went to the movies. My housekeeper would be here — five days a week — from nine until four, when I came home from work. This worked out beautifully.

As the disease progressed, I kept getting more information about it from every source I could. I'm a professional administrator, so I was going to administer this whole situation. But let me say that this was a joint effort, because I could never have done it alone. My husband and I decided to do it together. If I was down and said, "I can't stand it any more, let's look into a nursing home," he'd say, "Let's wait until tomorrow." And tomorrow, of course, you'd go on to another day, and you'd say, "Okay, I'll get through this."

Mother was in, as I said, the early stages when she came here, but she covered so beautifully. She took care of herself as she always did, so the first stages just came and went, with memory loss and some agitation, but nobody really paid any attention to them. She never talked about something being wrong with her. She must have just decided to live with it. Mother was a very strong woman, and wouldn't let anything defeat her. She never really became depressed, which is unusual for Alzheimer's patients.

We had a gerontologist come out to see mother one time. No matter how big your home is, they always say it isn't big enough for three generations. We looked at the woman and said, "We know what you mean, but you don't know where we're coming from." We had already thought of that. We had already thought of getting mother an apartment in the building, but I said, "That's ridiculous." So we agreed that it would work to have her in our apartment. We decided to do it together. It was the *we* that made it work. "We" was the magic word for us.

The first six months mother was here were difficult, because, all of a sudden we were the parents of a very strong, but confused, woman. It was a role reversal. She became our child and we became her parents. And it was practically impossible to convince her that being with us was good for her. It would be hard to convince me. I would hate it, too. I was still her child, but I had become her mother. Even though she was here in our home, mother constantly wanted to go back to her own home. She didn't want to go back to Florida, she wanted to go back to New York, where she was born. During this time, my mother kept expecting my father to come home for dinner, which was very hard to deal with, too.

During that first year, we felt that mother wanted to jump right out of her skin. Because that was the feeling we got, we tried to do a lot of entertaining, and planned a lot of special events for her. If she wanted to walk, we walked. If she wanted to go out on the weekend, we went. We were like the three musketeers. There was a period then I actually rubbed other people's nerves with the situation, because I refused to isolate her. We went out to dinner. We went to friends' houses. And if the friends didn't want us as a trio, we didn't go. I was very firm about this. I would never get a sitter at night while mother was still able to socialize. We always had people at our home. And my friends who really cared still came. We always entertained. I think we had two or three showers or parties of 25 or 35 while she was in the early stages.

One of the most difficult parts was the wandering — the wanting to run out of the house all the time. My husband and I would sleep in shifts. I'd go to sleep early and he'd stay up. Then he'd go to sleep and I'd get up. We didn't deadbolt the door or put double locks on the doors. We were afraid that, if the door was locked, she would jump out the window. That's how much she wanted to leave. Instead, we put cowbells on the door, so that when she started to go out of the door, we would hear her.

When mother was with us, we never left her out of our sight. Neither did the housekeeper; neither did any of our children who were here. Mother had eyes watching her everywhere. There was always one person with his eye on the door. When mother was here, we slept the way we slept when our children were small. It was the same kind of sleep. In addition to the wandering and the pacing and the sleepless nights, there were the questions. We were repeatedly asked the same questions.

One day, I had to get a sitter for mother, because my housekeeper couldn't come. Well, my mother just wouldn't stay with her, and so she disappeared. She ran out of the house. We don't know to this day where she went. Fortunately, we had known enough to get her a medical alert bracelet when she came to live with us. However, the bracelet indicated only memory loss. Remember that mother looked perfectly normal and healthy and young, so nobody would have stopped her.

She had disappeared at one o'clock, and at ten o'clock that night, a cabdriver somewhere stopped for her. Mother wanted to go north — she wanted to go home. She really wanted to go to New York, but the cab driver thought she wanted to go to the northern suburbs. She ran up a $56 cab bill. The cab driver finally called the police. When the police officer came, he saw the medical alert bracelet on her arm, called us, and had the cab driver bring her home. It was midnight when she got home. When she came in, we said, "What happened? Are you all right?" She said, "Boy, I had some day!"

At that time, my husband and I both worked during the day, and so we shared the responsibility for my mother. When we would get home from work in the afternoon, I would make dinner for mother. And Ed would feed her while I was getting our dinner ready. While I was doing the dishes, Ed would take her to the lobby and walk her around. Then Ed would bring her back up to the apartment to do whatever he had to do. Then I would give mother a bath, or whatever. We were constantly moving. There was no time when you would find the three of us sitting in the living room, reading the newspaper. If Ed was playing golf, I would take mother downtown — just for the bus ride. If I wanted to go somewhere, he would walk her around the building six or seven times. Perpetual motion, I call it.

Mother had boundless energy during that period. There

were some mornings that I would walk her around the building eight or nine times before the housekeeper came. Remember when it was 24° below zero a couple of years ago? Just try
and take an Alzheimer's patient outside in that kind of
weather. There were many times that I thought, "Maybe I'll
walk her around with her coat open. Maybe she'll develop
something." I didn't really wish her dead, but I wished it would
all be over. I would say, "God, I wish this restless period was
over," but I never would say I wished her dead. I didn't know
what I really wished for.

The middle stages of the disease were horrible. Mother
would get furious. She was combative, and she was constantly
pacing around. She'd do my dishes and, of course, she'd put
the dishes in the refrigerator, thinking it was the dishwasher.
One night mother was washing something, and she was washing it with furniture polish. I must have grabbed at her, and I
said, "Put that down!!!!!" She went into her room crying. And
I was standing there in the kitchen, crying. But then I realized
that she would come out in another second and not remember
what had happened. And, of course, she came out and didn't
remember.

Naturally, your instincts are to yell or scream at them. I
never really yelled at her, which is why Ed and I yelled at each
other. That was wonderful to be able to do. It was incredible
for my husband to go along with this as he did. Even though
she was always telling him to do this or do that, he kept right
on helping me care for her. He was even helping me diaper
her, when I couldn't lift her any more. I don't think I could
have done all of what I did if it had been my mother-in-law, instead of my mother.

We never did have to have around-the-clock nursing for
mother. We used our housekeeper right to the end. She was
here during the day, and we took over in the evening. When
we wanted to go out on the weekend, or take a mini-weekend,
I asked an LPN I had known for years to come and stay with

mother. It was expensive, but it was certainly worth it. There is really nothing to do in caring for the patient during the last stages.

When all of the walking stopped and when the talking finally stopped, it became easier for us to take care of her. She wasn't running, she wasn't raving, she wasn't combative. She seemed to be content. For me, it was over then. It was over, maybe, because it wasn't that difficult any more. I think mother was a vegetable for about four months before she died. We had to feed her and she didn't walk and she didn't talk. But she was still out of bed every day.

The only thing that really bothered me during the period — as I said on television — was the first time I had to diaper my mother. That was the saddest day of my life. I'll never forget the feeling I had the first time. I thought, "Here is this woman who took care of me, who diapered me, and now I'm diapering her." I didn't feel as sad any other time as I did then.

Being able to take care of an Alzheimer's patient at home depends on your circumstances. It depends on whether you have small children — or even teenagers — in the house who need your attention. You can't work both ends. I really don't believe I could have done it if I had teenagers in the house. It was just too time consuming. You also need help — a sibling or spouse — who will work with you. You can't do it alone. What we did was right for us at that time. If mother had lived for more than two years, who knows? She could be in a nursing home right now.

Early on, my husband and I made a pact that we would let mother die at home, if we could. And we did. I said, "I think she's dead." And Ed said, "What do you want to do?" I said, "Let's have a drink." Afterwards, I called the doctor and said, "I believe mother's dead." We had already told the doctor that we didn't want any heroics. We wanted her to die at home. She did, and it was very peaceful. Mother died of an embolism in the lung, perhaps from not talking — who knows?

We called the police and did everything you're supposed to do when someone has died at home. It so happened that the policeman who came was the one who came the night mother disappeared. By that time, we had developed a relationship. The policeman knew about mother and knew about our story. There had been an article with mother's picture in the Sun Times that summer.

Even though we knew exactly what we were going to do when she died, and even though we were so calm about it, an amazing thing happened. For about eight months after her death, I had nightmares at least once a month. And you know what those nightmares were? That she was here. I'd wake up screaming and shaking, because I *knew* she was here. (Some pyschiatrist would have a terrific time with that.) In my dreams, she was either calling me or going somewhere, and I would wake up scared to death. Either I saw her in the bathroom doing something to the tub or in the kitchen or in her room.

The nightmares went away after about eight months, but every month before that I would have them. When I said to different people, "Boy, I had another one," they'd say, "What was it this time?" And I'd say, "She was in her room." Then the nightmares disappeared, and I haven't had one since. Subconsciously, the fear was that she was back and it wasn't over yet. When I told that to some of the professionals, they said, "Oh boy, is that wonderful to know, because you were so calm and you handled it and, suddenly, bingo, you're screaming." Everybody has something like this happen — whether it's while they're going through the ordeal or afterwards. It does take a toll.

I consider myself one of the lucky ones, because it was all over so quickly. Two years is really a very short time. We did feel, however, that if things went along for an indefinite period, of course, we would have had to put her in a nursing home. We would have had to put her in a nursing home to save ourselves. But for those two years, we managed. And we have no regrets. It would have cost us a lot of money to add enough to her pension to keep her in a nursing home.

I was always amazed that my children didn't give me any flack about caring for mother at home. They never said, "Why don't you and dad put her in a nursing home?" They never said that to us. We used to talk about that all the time, because it would be natural for the children to say, "Look what's happening to you two." The classic remark, however, was made by my youngest daughter on a dinner date after my mother had died. The young man had asked, "Did your grandma leave you anything?" And my daughter said, "Yes, she left my mother and father in good health." When my daughter came home, she said, "You can't believe what I said to Bernie tonight. I really let him have it!" That was incredible. This whole thing was a learning experience.

I'm glad that my whole family grew with the experience and that it did some wonderful things. We talk about the positive side of coping. I'm a living example that there is a positive side. I hear the kids talk about the experience among themselves. They're all in their twenties now. And it's amazing. I sit there and hear them talking and I don't realize they're talking about their own family. You'd think they were talking about something they had seen on television the night before.

After mother's death, the children were so conscious of caring for an older person and of family ties that we would get a call from one of them every other week, once a week, twice a week, or whatever. "Hi, what's new? We're coming in for the weekend." Every time we sneezed, somebody was coming home. The experience raised their awareness of the family unit. When my husband and I spoke at one of the medical centers recently, someone asked us, "What do you think your children would do, given the same situation?" And I said, "I don't have any question in my mind but what they would take care of us." Our children reflect our own feelings.

Mother will have been dead two years in August. And though she's gone, I'm still very involved in the National Association of Alzheimer's and Related Diseases. I'm president of the Chicago chapter. I resigned my job at the Temple, so that I could devote myself to this organization.

You see, I have this little crusade, which my husband calls my "Eleanor Roosevelt syndrome." When my mother first came here, I took her to three day care centers, and asked if she could come there while I was at work. And they all said, "No, we're sorry, we don't take anyone with 'that' disease. We can't be responsible for her wandering or for her mood swings," or whatever. I was furious that day care centers would not take her.

During my administration, our chapter of the Alzheimer's Association will be developing a day care center for Alzheimer's patients only — even though a lot of centers are taking Alzheimer's patients now. And the centers that do take them are learning. They really are. But I'll never forget what I faced when mother was in a condition where she really could have stayed in a day care center and been productive. So day care is really my highest priority. That's what my Eleanor Roosevelt syndrome is. I have so much to do and so little time to do it.

We have 1600 members in our group. And we're adding 50 new members each month. When I started, there were 324 members. Acutally, I have been able to bring people *back* into the group. When I started working with the organization, people said, "I'm done with this damned disease, I never want to hear its name. Just leave me alone!" Now, they're saying, "Is there anything we can do? It's all over, so we want to help." They want to help because they feel that, until we know what causes Alzheimer's disease, their families are in jeopardy. They're not doing it for the patient who died, but for themselves and their children. My experience scared me — scared me for myself, but mostly for my kids.

Alzheimer's has become a very fashionable disease. Everybody knows somebody who either has Alzheimer's or may have it. And everybody is coming to me — radio and television reporters, etc. Writers call, wanting to sell stories. All of a sudden, we have stars involved. Rita Hayworth's daughter, Yasmin, constantly works for Alzheimer's. We didn't have celebrities before, but now all of a sudden, we have celebrities. The president of Westinghouse Television just died. He had contracted the disease at 61. And now, there are all kinds of tapes coming out of Westinghouse — with stars doing them — about our disease.

Our national Alzheimer's organization is lobbying in Washington. We hope that three things might happen as a result. We hope that Medicare will provide some coverage for custodial care. We don't know what it will be, but they're talking about it now. We're also hoping that there will be a tax deduction for the care of a dependent parent. Right now, it's between a rock and a hard place with the government. Our organization is only five years old, but we've come a long way.

My first responsibility, as president of the Chicago chapter, is to the families who are now going through what I went through. Every case is so different. They say there are five stages, but you can go from stage one to stage five, never hitting, two, three, or four. My mother went from stage one to stage three and then back to stage one, when she seemed to be getting better.

The first stage of the disease is denial and some loss of recent memory. The second stage reflects the inability to understand money matters, irritability, and depression. The third stage usually includes wandering, acute depression, inability to remember family names, inability to read. The fourth stage includes the inability to cope with the daily rhythms, inability to feed self, a total loss of recent memory, incontinence, inability to find your way, and lack of recognition of individuals. The fifth stage in when everything shuts down.

I feel comfortable with the way we handled the situation, and I have no regrets. Did either of us have an emotional letdown after my mother died? I think my husband did. He has this wonderful desire to be needed, and afterwards, I wasn't saying to him, "Stay home for a while, will you, I have to go to the grocery store." Or, "Will you please help me?" or, "I need you for this." I think it really was a letdown for him — the letdown of feeling that he wasn't needed. He knew he had been so much needed when mother was with us.

He's recovered now, because I have him working with me on chapter projects. We go out and speak together, for example. It's been a wonderful catharsis for us. We talk to a lot of groups. We tell the people how we handled having my mother in our home. Although we tell people that this arrangement worked for us, we also tell them that "It doesn't work for everyone."

WHY? BECAUSE SOMEONE
HAD TO DO IT!

For James Walters assuming responsibility for his wife's friend, Edna, was not a new experience. He had been through it all with his own mother. He knew the ups and downs, the ins and outs, and a lot of the problems of the elderly. What Jim wasn't prepared for was an over zealous judge with a seemingly punitive attitude.

Edna Anderson, who is about 72 years old now, is a friend of my wife — has been for many years. I met her through Liz when we were married, seven or eight years ago.

When I met her, she was very active. Edna was a writer, and she did freelance work for a community newspaper and public relations for several restaurants. She also did an excellent newspaper column about the goings on in this city — restaurants, theater, special events. Incidentally, she was also a good cook and liked to entertain. At that time, Edna was really quite an aggressive woman. In fact, she was very, very pushy. And I thought her a pain in the neck.

Edna's father, who managed farms upstate, died about eight years ago, leaving a fairly decent estate. Her mother had died a few years before her father, and the only other member of the family is a sister on the West Coast. Her sister, whom we call Sis, was married to a career army officer, her husband having died a couple of years after his retirement. Sis is an invalid, in so many respects, that it is hard to imagine that she lives by herself, gets around, drives a car, runs a ceramics class, and has all sorts of activities. Edna is probably two years older than her sister.

For a while, Liz and I saw or talked to Edna several times a month. Then we began to see less of her. We didn't have as much contact for some reason. Don't really know why. Liz did, however, talk to her on the phone from time to time. During these conversations, Liz began to recognize that she — Edna — was getting into a state of depression. Well, somehow or other, Liz managed to talk Edna into going over to the local hospital. I guess they have an outpatient psychiatric department, or something like that. And Edna did go there for a while. But she didn't go there long enough — that's really quite certain.

Somewhere along the line after that, Edna complained to Liz about having trouble with her writing. She was a prolific writer, but all of a sudden, the flow stopped. I know that, several times, Liz went over and did articles for her, using the information Edna had, generally. I guess this must have happened three or four times. We both tried to persuade Edna "to get with it." But she just didn't have the get up and go to start writing. She just couldn't get going.

This was also the time when we noticed that she was starting to lose weight. When I first met her, Edna weighed around 140 or 150 pounds and was about 5' 8". So when she got down to 125 - 130 pounds there was a very noticeable difference. She was always very well dressed and her make-up was always just so. But now, her clothes didn't fit as they should. Also, she wasn't quite up to par in her personal care, because she started to look a little bit tatty — which was very unusual. As I said earlier, she was usually well made up. She had a great head of red hair and always had it well done. I think it was pink at one time, which really rattled me.

We are now coming up to the early part of 1980. We knew that Edna wasn't doing all that well. We were having her over for dinner from time to time — more often that we had in the past — and she would eat voraciously, to put it mildly. We learned, about that time, that she was not eating at home, because "she didn't want to shop." She wouldn't use her car to go out shopping. She didn't want to use the stove, for fear she would mar it and the landlord would make her pay for it. At

the same time, Edna was becoming more and more with-
drawn.

On Good Friday of 1980, Liz received a call from a woman
who was Edna's neighbor. Her neighbor was a nursing super-
visor at Cedars Hospital. Apparently, Edna had called her.
The woman came into her apartment and found Edna quite
emaciated — really in horrible shape. The neighbor managed
to get our friend over to the hospital and then got in touch with
her doctor, who came over and examined her. The doctor
found she was definitely in a state of malnutrition. She also
had a bad heart, but this she knew. It was something she was
being treated for.

At this time, Edna was also very fearful. She was paranoid
with regard to anything and everything. We first noticed the
paranoia when she told us she was sure that federal agents
were after her — the IRS. Although they were not after her at
the time, she had reason to assume that they might be, because
she hadn't been paying her taxes. Edna believed the IRS was
listening to her through her TV set and on the telephone. She
was so sure about it that she called Liz one morning to ask if
she had heard the news over the radio.

But back to Easter weekend, when Edna went to the hospital. After her internist examined her, he called in a psychiatrist, one Dr. Jose Gonzalez. Dr. Gonzalez was to be of great
help to Edna and to my wife and me from that point on.

When Edna was able to leave Cedars Hospital, she was
transferred to Kensington, a psychiatric hospital. When she
was at Kensington, it was the same thing. The IRS and everybody at Kensington was listening to her. They wanted to know
how much money she had. They wanted to know this and that.
But, of course, they didn't really.

Edna was, I think, well taken care of at Kensington, where
she was on a secured floor. She was very fortunate in having
gotten Dr. Gonzalez, because that man was really a caring person. I guess he was seeing her every other day — probably

more than that. And I got to know him. We get along well. And that has worked out to Edna's advantage. He did a meticulous job, I felt, working with her medication to make sure things were going right — that she wasn't getting too much or too little medication. After about six months, Gonzalez said she could leave. She could leave the hospital and see how she could make it on her own.

At that point, she was improving all the time. Really, she was quite lucid and quite "with it" a lot of the time. She had kept up with current events on TV, and I guess she read newspapers once in a while and she did read some magazines. On the surface, at least, it looked like maybe she would be able to hack it.

After she left the hospital, Edna stayed with us for about the first two or three weeks. She had the guest room and that was all there was to that. Edna really wanted us to take care of her in our own home. She wanted to move in with us. Her very remote second choice was her own apartment. While she was in the hospital, we had taken her out on passes — several times. Every time we brought her here — I guess, probably, four times — she didn't want to go back to that hospital.

Finally, we persuaded her to go back to her apartment to see how well she could do. She was driving Liz wacky, because Liz was with her all of the time. Well, of course, there wasn't anything in the apartment, in terms of food. So the first thing was, I took her shopping at the local grocery store, which is where I shop. And I pretty well stocked her up. I got her the kind of things that made it possible for her to open a can and have a meal. She wasn't going to build any kind of a real meal at all. There was just no way. I also got the smallest cuts of meat I could, and things like that. I had her stocked up for about ten days at least. What I got wasn't exactly exotic stuff, but at least it was nutritious, and she wasn't going to be on a corn flake diet or something like that — which she was wont to do.

Unfortunately, Edna still wouldn't use the stove. And she was also fearful of using the refrigerator. In fact, I went over there one time and she said she couldn't use the freezer. "Why can't you use use the freezer?" "Well, it's all iced up. It needs to be defrosted." And, boy, it was! It had three inches of ice in there. I simply attacked it, and got all the ice out. She was having fits! "You're going to ruin it. You're going to scratch it. The landlord is going to cause me to pay for a refrigerator. And I can't afford it." So, she didn't want to use the refrigerator; she didn't want to use the stove.

Since she wasn't cooking, I stocked her up with the can opener sorts of things. In fact, we bought her a can opener. We also bought her TV dinners, because she liked those. She didn't want to put them in the oven. She would rather let them thaw and eat them cold, I think. We had also suggested to her the possibility of Meals on Wheels or even making an arrangement with one of her neighbors to provide meals for her. But she wasn't having any of the first and we couldn't work the other one out.

Sometime before Edna went to the hospital that first time, Liz had made a quick trip over to her apartment, because Edna hadn't answered the phone all day, and Liz was afraid something had happened to her. Edna was in such bad shape that Liz feared for the worst. She arranged immediately for power of attorney, so that we could keep things going in an emergency. Liz also arranged for a key to her safety deposit box, where Edna had put family jewelry and important papers.

I gave Edna back the checkbook I had used to pay her bills. And she was managing — somewhat — to pay things. She paid her telephone bill, she paid the rent — the things that came due regularly, she kept up with. I don't know about the other things.

Edna wouldn't go out and get her hair done or anything. She wouldn't do any shopping. I was doing the weekly shop-

ping and bringing it over to her. We were also picking her up,
bringing her here, doing her shopping, and taking her home.
We would bring her here for dinner and then shop on the way
back. Edna just couldn't make up her mind about anything.
She couldn't even make up her mind about such things as the
kind of bread she wanted. I got so I didn't bother any more, I
simply did the shopping to make sure it was done. And that
was that.

Edna continued to be in a depressed state after she moved
back to her apartment. From time to time, she would say it
would be better for everybody, if "I just went down the drain." I
knew she wasn't capable of committing suicide, because she
wouldn't be able to make up her mind how to do it. She also,
unfortunately, was not taking her medication regularly. At that
time, the psychiatrist wanted to see her monthly. And I made
sure that did take place. On at least one occasion, when she
didn't want to go to the doctor, I had threatened to carry her if
that was the only way I was going to get her there.

Edna got out of the psychiatric hospital in May of 1980.
And she was back in the hospital in November. She went back
in the hospital because I had made an appointment for her to
see Dr. Gonzalez at Kensington. Liz went with me. It was a
late afternoon appointment. When we brought her in there,
she really looked bad. She was probably down to less than 100
pounds.

Anyway, her physical condition was such that Gonzalez
wanted to put her back in Cedars Hospital, but they didn't
have a room. Dr. Gonzalez then managed to get her a room at
Kensington, because he's a fairly big man there. But Edna said
she would not sign the admission papers. So Dr. Gonzalez
said, "Well now look, I can legally commit you to the hospital.
On my say so, they will take you in." He also told her that if she
signed the papers herself, she would be free to sign herself out
after five days — that is, after giving five days notice. Edna
finally agreed to enter the hospital — with no little bit of coax-

ing from us. It took more than 45 minutes to get her to sign the papers. We went there in the late afternoon and we didn't leave until nine o'clock that night.

After this hospitalization, Gonzalez said, "Forget it, she can't take care of herself." That was very apparent. Liz and I decided, then, that we ought to get her into a retirement hotel — for openers. At least she would have a room, somebody to take care of the place, and she would get her meals. We finally chose Lexington House. It was not a luxury place by any means, but it was adequate. It was also on a street where Edna had lived many, many years ago. We felt that since it was a familiar neighborhood, she would, indeed, get out and get around a little bit. Also, Lexington House was not far from our home. As a matter of fact, it was within walking distance — albeit a long walk.

Edna went into Lexington House in mid-January, I think, and she was managing fairly well. She never really went out of the place, though, unless somebody was with her — "somebody" being Liz or myself. The Lexington House staff was also going to see that Edna got her medication. They said they would watch to see that she took it, but they could not dispense it to her. They could suggest that she take her medication, but if she didn't, they couldn't do anything about it.

To give you an idea of how Edna was doing at this point Edna wouldn't have a telephone in her room, although she could have. She could have had a hot plate and a refrigerator too, if she had wanted them. But she just couldn't cope. We brought writing materials to her. She didn't write. She didn't want her typewriter, she didn't want her TV, and so forth. She wouldn't even hang pictures on the wall. She had two suitcases, a few bits of outerwear and, of course, a few pieces of clothing. For the most part, she was wearing a pair of slacks, as well as a skirt — even when it was warm.

Perhaps I should give you a little background concerning my involvement in this situation. My mother, after my father died, began to deteriorate in much the same way as Edna. I didn't really recognize it to begin with. This was in 1963, I believe. My mother's name was also Edna, by the way. Mother was in kind of bad shape. I started to recognize this when I visited her.

My mother had never driven a car before in her life. She learned to drive after my father died and she did, indeed, manage to get around pretty well. For a while after dad died, mother worked as a telephone operator. Then, for whatever reason — probably because she was 65 and getting her social security — she decided to stop working. Fine. Not that she had a hellishly big income — as I found out later. Somewhere along the line, mother said, "Living in this house alone, I would like to have a dog." So we got a dog for her from some animal shelter. Then she had the terrible misfortune of the dog becoming ill and having to be put away. And you can imagine how that affected a person in her state. So that was the beginning.

As she started to get in worse and worse shape, she decided she was going to sell the house. And she did it. She did it in such a way that I didn't have anything to do with it. And she got taken. She got a pitifully small amount for a five-room, frame bungalow, on a double corner lot. There wasn't a thing I could do. I was infuriated, not at her, because she didn't know what she was doing, but at the people who took her. At that stage, I got her an apartment on the northwest side, where we had lived at one time and where I had gone through school. While she was in this apartment, my mother started to get into the kind of thing that Edna was in, except that my mother, at least, would cook. In fact, she invited my exwife and myself over for Thangsgiving dinner. Now my mother was a darned good cook, but you would never have known it from that meal. Things were burned, things were uncooked. The whole bit. It was just a diaster! We left as gracefully as possible.

At the same time, I got to looking into her bank account

and what not. I managed to find an account she had at Central Trust and set up a joint signature account with her there. I also arranged for the bank to send her $125 every two weeks for her maintenance. I guess the corker in this situation was the time that she took the $125 she received from the bank and gave it to somebody out on the street.

There came the time when I got in touch with mother's younger sister, and said, "Hey, there is a problem." Ultimately, we got my mother into Oakdale psychiatric hospital for tests. As it turned out, she had blockage of the blood to the brain. From then on, it was all down hill.

After her stay at Oakdale I had to put mother in a state insitution. The facility was not all that bad. It was strictly a warehouse kind of thing, no matter how you look at it. But they did feed her; they did care for her. And they did steal everything they could from her.

Mother was in the state institution for about two years — maybe a little bit longer, but not much longer. I went out there, with her sister, every week for the first couple of months. As she deteriorated, we went out less often. Since my mother liked pineapple milk shakes, we would stop at the local milk shakery and bring one in for her. They had the buddy system there, so we'd bring one for her buddy at the same time. Every time we went out there, we brought her that milkshake, even though, toward the end, she didn't even recognize us. But she still loved that milkshake. Ultimately, she died there. She was bedridden at the time, had been for some while, so I was expecting it. And she simply expired — probably all for the best. I was informed by telephone.

This experience is probably why I was capable of, and willing to, deal with Edna Anderson. Since I had been thru this experience with my mother, I knew what would happen. Edna didn't have relative one in this area. If she were to go on the public dole, it would have been hard on her, because she still recognized certain things that were happening around her. She was not completely out of touch with reality, so it would really have racked her up. It probably would have caused her to have more problems than she does now.

During Edna's hospital stays, I began to find out just what money she did have. Although we thought she was just a few rungs from the poverty level, that was hardly the case, I discovered. Her father had been an astute investor. So Edna really has a pretty good thing going for her. She had an income that would keep her independent, and is keeping her independent to this day, and will into the foreseeable future.

Edna went into the hospital one more time. And she went with the same reluctance she had every other time. By now, we knew darned well that she couldn't go back to her apartment. She could not go back to Lexington House. We had kept the apartment all of the time, hoping, for her sake, that she could get back in there and hack it. But she couldn't. And this was very obvious to everyone concerned — except, of course, Edna.

So I said, "Okay, we're going to have to get Edna into a nursing home and we're going to have to clean out this apartment. That's all, period. We're going to have to take over. At that point, we decided that I was going to become her legal guardian. Of course, she resisted that to begin with, even though she had asked — a number of times — if I would take over her affairs. But she just didn't like the idea of the *legal* guardianship. She really didn't want me to know anything about her affairs. She's an intensely private person.

Liz took the task of finding a nursing home. And I took the task of doing whatever I could to get the apartment cleared up. Then, of course, we both went at it. But that apartment was wall-to-wall shopping bags, with a narrow path running through each room. In addition to the shopping bags, there were all kinds of boxes filled with papers, cash, clothing, gifts that she never even opened, and so forth. One of the first things I did when I was closing out Edna's apartment was to go to the postoffice and have her address changed to my home address. In that way, I could, at least, get a handle on what stocks and bonds she had from the dividend checks that came in.

We closed out Edna's apartment and put her things in storage here. There are also some things in storage in her home state that are part of the furnishings of the family home. Edna owns them, but she'll probably never see them again. I'm going to send them to her sister on the west coast because her sister wants them. The stuff that's here is stored nearby. I expect the court to say, one day, "Get rid of that stuff. Don't be paying a thousand dollars or so for storage and insurance on things that really aren't worth all that much." For Edna that is her lifeline, a necessary security blanket, and she asks about them from time to time. And we didn't want to burn all her bridges.

It was in April of 1982 when these things took place. Then in May or June of that year, I went through court and legally became guardian of her estate, with Liz as guardian of her person. During the first year after I became Edna's guardian, I spent many, many hours just going through the stuff that we had already culled. We went through every one of those bags that had been in her apartment. We had gone through a lot of them at the apartment so we didn't have to move them. But we did take those that were pertinent, brought them here to the house, and put them in my office. I then went through them with a fine-tooth comb.

Finally, the nickles and dimes and the collections of quarters and dollar bills and ten dollar bills began to surface. The trouble with going through this bag routine is that you have to open every envelope and flip through every page. I have no idea how much money I threw away. I'm sure I threw some away. But I just can't do anything about it. People are very sly, they put things in strange places — in a safe place for safe keeping. But it's so safe, it's under the paper used to line the drawers, and all of those good places.

As I said, we had to find a nursing home for Edna. My wife started looking for a home for her. And we took her to see three of them. Edna was not interested when she saw people on walkers or in wheelchairs. That is depressing. That's going to affect you and me as well as anybody else. She could only see that this was going to be her condition sometime in the future. As it is so far, that is not her condition. But anyway, she finally said, "Well all right."

We were pleased with the one Edna chose until it changed ownership. Now, I think, there are some subtle things happening there that we are going to have to look into further. We have never really stopped investigating nursing homes. At the moment, she is at the lowest level of care. In other words, it's effectively room and board and take your medication. She is watched. There is a nursing staff on board, there's a doctor available. So, it's exactly what she needs. The food is decent. The place is relatively clean. She complains bitterly at times. Liz originally thought Edna should have a single room, but my thoughts were that she would be better off with a double room. And the psychiatrist agreed with me. She did have a roommate that she formed a friendship with. However, when my wife suggests that the two of them look at other homes, Edna isn't interested. Dr. Gonzalez still sees her every four to six weeks. He goes there to see her. One of the nice things about that place is that it is between the hospital and the doctor's home.

Edna is surviving. Her condition is neither noticeably better nor noticeably worse. Sometimes she's clear and lucid, and sometimes she's not. She's still paranoid and she's afraid that she doesn't have enough money to pay for the home, and she's sure that they are going to toss her out.

We take Edna out for lunch or dinner from time to time, and we always try to get her to come to our home for Christmas and Easter and for other special events. But it's harder and harder to get her to leave the nursing home.

But now to the legal things and to the problems involved —

problems that often cause me to have second thoughts about guardianship. Things are very different if you are not a member of the family.

I contacted my attorney in the spring of 1982 to see what was involved in becoming a legal guardian. First off, I had to get statements from her psychiatrist and from her internist to the effect that she was not competent to care for herself. It wasn't that she was a raving maniac or anything. She was just totally paranoid and she couldn't make any decisions — what she wanted to wear or what she wanted to order in a restaurant.

Then I found that the court would want a complete accounting of what she owned — stocks, bonds, CDs, money market funds, and bank accounts. And, at this time, we weren't even sure we had found everything she had stashed away. Edna didn't like this because she was a very private person and she really didn't want me poking around in her affairs — even though she had asked me on several occasions to take charge of everything if it became necessary.

I had already been writing down expenditures in a sort of diary that I kept, to have some idea of what events took place and when. This was to cover myself, so that I could say, "Hey, I spent the money for this or I did that." Or, "We went here." Or, "We spent money for Edna's clothing." "Liz took Edna out for lunch and shopping." Or, "They went to the ophthalmologist. They took a taxi, because Liz couldn't take the car and Edna was too frail to take a bus." But getting this all together, in the form wanted, was a miserable chore.

The court named an attorney to represent Edna — a woman who worked in probate almost exclusively, and really knew what she was doing. The attorney talked to Edna before we all had to appear in court — all but Edna, although she could have appeared if she had wanted to. Edna's attorney took all of the information I had provided with respect to monies that I had spent from the account and so on. She needed this information because she had to give her recommendation to the judge when we finally went into court.

The process of appearing in court for this plenary guardianship was really not much at all. The attorney representing me, who was an assistant to the man I really wanted, presented the case. Then Edna's attorney made her report and, as agreed upon earlier, recommended that I become guardian of Edna's estate and that my wife be guardian of her person. She had suggested that because Edna was concerned my wife was not involved.

The judge ruled, and that was about all there was to that. The judge did, however, ask Edna's attorney to continue to represent her for several months at least. I was glad about that because, from time to time, Edna would say, "I don't have any money. How are you paying for this? How are my bills being paid?" So when that happened, Edna's attorney would speak to Edna, answer any questions she had, and try to put her mind at ease. I also encouraged Edna to call her attorney if she had any questions.

Another responsibility of a legal guardian is to report, annually, to the probate judge, who had to be satisfied that you are handling the estate properly. When the time of the first accounting came up, my attorney and I proceeded in very much the same way as we had when I applied for guardianship — thinking that we would go up before the same probate judge.

As it turned out, we got a different judge — one who was really quite persnickety. He asked all sorts of questions. He gave me fits. I was ready to throw in the towel right then and there, because this man was asking that information be recorded and reported in an entirely different way than the first judge had wanted it. This simply meant that I had to tear my filing system apart and put it back together again. And I had to charge Edna for all of that time.

The judge also second guessed me and a prominent lady investment counselor who had been an advisor to at least two presidents of the United States that I know of. She was a very close friend of Edna's and acting during this period as her financial advisor on a pro bono basis. For example, among Edna's holdings were a tax free municipal bond account and a money fund account together totaling approximately $50,000. And they were earning a bit over 8% interest. A good rate at the time. Since these were uninsured accounts, the judge ordered me to convert them to something that was insured. So I had to cancel the two accounts and put the money in a 5-½% savings account. There's now $50,000 in the account and it is earning only $2500 per year. Early on, I had found $35,000 in some out of the way savings and loan, where it was earning 5%, and I took it out of there because it wasn't making enough money for Edna. So now, we're back to square one. It's ridiculous!

The judge also said that I had been charging too much for my time, and that it should be cut by one-third. He also ordered me to pay the difference — some $800 — back to the estate. This also gave me fits, because my lawyer thought that I was not charging enough. Of course the judge did not question the hourly rate of our lawyer's assistant, which was about eight times more — for an assistant, yet.

When you're a legal guardian, it seems that everything you do has to be approved by the court. We were told that if we wanted to move Edna to a different nursing home, we would have to justify it, not only in terms of the money — either more or less — but also in terms of the quality of care. As if the judge knew or cared anything about that! And if you want to do something with the estate, you have to get permission of the court. I can't see that. I think of all the money that has to be spent on legal fees, just to get another 1% or 2% interest, and it just doesn't seem worth it. Of course this is all supposed to be in Edna's best interest. But, strangely enough, the second judge didn't even ask anything about Edna or her condition. She was an estate to him, not a person.

We've heard from time to time that judges in this city have been known to squeeze out the guardian of a relatively large estate — which this one is — so he can pass it along to a friend who, you may be sure is not going to handle it for a modest fee.

Now, I'm on my third attorney and have yet to make my second report to the probate judge. Somehow, attorneys just don't seem to care. I guess because it's my neck on the line, not theirs. Needless to say, I've lost a lot of zeal for this arrangement. More than once, I've been ready to bail out. But every time I get to that point, Edna's psychiatrist urges me not to do so. He tell's me that I am one of only four people in this world that Edna trusts. Of those four the only one who could or would take over with her blessing would be Liz and then I'd still be involved. So I ask you, where do I go from here?

NOT UNTIL YOU'VE BEEN THERE

A professional social worker — experienced in the field of aging — Leah Goldman — found that her mother's physical and mental deterioration was a situation in which she, herself, profited from professional help.

At the time, Leah did not get, from many of her friends and relatives, the understanding, support, and affirmation of her own feelings, which are so necessary. As a result of going through this wrenching experience, Leah now relates to those she counsels — particularly daughters — in a way she never did before.

Here, she shares her feelings and reactions with candor and eloquence.

My mother and father lived in New York. Prior to 1971, when my father died, my mother was doing okay, although she was showing some signs of senility. During that time mother and dad had had a sort of cup and saucer relationship, in which he would move very quickly into a situation in a kind of anticipatory way. When we were visiting, for example, I remember him saying, "Now don't forget the potatoes," or "Check the potatoes in the oven," or "When you're coming out of the kitchen, bring the salt." And he did that rather nicely. What he was doing was not apparent to other people, and wasn't even apparent to her, I think.

My dad was close to 80 when he died; my mother was 73. The last time that I was at home in New York for any length of time — about six weeks, I'd say — was when he was in the hospital just before he died. I could see how very shaky mother was then. We were going up to the hospital every day, and she could manage getting there by train. She also did shopping, and she did food preparation. But there were soft spots. There were gaps in her behavior and there was a lot of repetition. She was also very unsure of herself, which was strange for a woman who had been extremely self-confident all of her life. I supposed that her behavior was partly due to concern about my father, but she just was not functioning too well.

After my father died, mother was on her own. She had a sister who lived a few blocks away from her. Her sister came in and helped out, from time to time, but she got sick and went to live with her daughter on Staten Island. So she was not available any more. Mother also had a sister-in-law, my Aunt Gertie, who was in the neighborhood. Aunt Gertie did what she could, but the situation wasn't good.

During that period, I was getting telephone calls from my mother — a lot of phone calls from her. "I got this letter," she would say, and then she would read me the letter she had gotten from the bank or from an investment house, some place like that. But she really didn't know what to make of the letter. I then began getting calls from the neighbors, the janitor of the building — people like that — telling me about the strange things she was doing. You see, mother was very involved with money. She was going to the bank every 20 minutes, putting money in and taking it out. Fortunately, it was a neighborhood bank and they knew her. I was going to New York a lot, trying to pull things together.

Mother was coming to visit me a lot at that time. She would come, supposedly for a week or two, and then she would stay week after week after week. I do have a brother, but she had a bad relationship with him. He's in Maryland, near Washington. But even if he had been in New York, it wouldn't have made too much difference. My mother and my brother were pretty well estranged. So she was coming out here.

From '71, when my father died, to '73, when my husband Lou died, mother was constantly running back and forth. She would come here and stay a while, then she would get restless and she would go back home. Then she would come back again and stay some length of time. When Lou had his first heart attack, my mother was here, which was unfortunate. And she was very, very upset about his illness. She would come to the hospital with me to visit, but she wasn't a good visitor. She just made things harder for me and for Lou, but her intentions were so goddamn good.

Of course after Lou died, she stayed on here. It was very difficult for me when she was here. She could take care of herself, so I could go off to work and leave her. She wasn't that bad, but she was unreliable. The mail would come, and I might not see it for three days. She had put it away somewhere. There were a lot of very, very irritating things that happened at that time.

While she was with me, she was also being very, very active in the neighborhood. She joined a seniors' group of some sort that met every other Friday, and she was very popular there. She went there very regularly. Mother looked terrific. She dressed beautifully, bathed every day, and her make-up and nails were always perfect. She also walked a lot, and she could walk all around the neighborhood without getting lost.

Somewhere along the line, we finally closed up her apartment in New York. It had become clear that she was not ever going to go back and stay there. She had gone back once, and it had been a disaster. So we had to go east and close up the apartment. That was a terrible time. She wanted to bring everything with her, and she couldn't understand why I didn't want all of the beautiful furniture. She had gorgeous stuff. It really was. It was beautiful. But she couldn't understand that I had a bed room all furnished. And a living room and a dining room. I did take some of the furniture. I took as much as I could, and I took her china. I'll never forget the packing. As fast as I put things into a barrel, she was taking them out. It was a nightmare. It was an absolute nightmare! During this time, she also had a kind of paranoid episode. She thought everything was missing — that it had all been stolen.

At any rate, we finally got that done, and then she came here to stay. I thought at one time, that she could live in a retirement hotel, so we looked at retirement hotels. But she really could not manage to live alone. She was afraid at night. So she just stayed home with me. Mother made friends very quickly, but most of her relationships were fairly superficial. In many ways, my mother was a very superficial person. Her emotional investment was mainly in her family — that is, her sisters. Mother had been in business all her life, so most of the people she knew, she knew through work. Socially, my mother never had a woman friend — a close friend. She didn't have that kind of network. But, as I said, mother was very, very popular. People used to call her, the ladies used to call her and they used to come by for her. It was superficial, but she didn't feel that. Mother didn't miss anybody from New York, except, perhaps, my Aunt Gertie. They talked to each other on the phone quite often, and they wrote letters to each other.

Mother was a very sociable person. When we would go shopping at the grocery store, very quickly I would find her in the green beans chatting with someone — not always a terribly appropriate thing to do. If there were two people stuck in an elevator, and my mother was one of them, she would be the first one to say something. She was also the type of person who would never sit next to someone on an airplane without striking up a conversation with them. It used to be that if the person indicated that he wasn't interested in conversation, my mother would know enough to back off. As she got older, however, she wouldn't pick up on the lack of interest. Sometimes I would see her talking to people who were dying to get away from her — and she not being aware of this at all.

Over a period of time, things just deteriorated and deteriorated and deteriorated. She was not able to go to the senior citizens' center any more. If she did manage to get there, somebody would usually call me at work and tell me that someone would have to come and take her home. She would also go for a walk in the neighborhood and get lost.

I was going to work every day, so there was nobody home with her. I was terrified that she would do some damage either to herself or to the house while I was at work. I used to dread coming home. During that period, I hated to have the work day end, because coming home was not coming home to relax. I had to watch her every moment. And what was I watching? I was watching to see that, if she picked up a piece of paper of mine, it wouldn't disappear or to see that she wouldn't take the coffee and put it in the laundry chute or something of that sort. I could drive myself crazy looking for the paper or the coffee or cleaning up after finding ice cream up on top of the refrigerator because mother had taken it out of the freezer and didn't know where to put it back. There were so many things. She put things into the garbage disposal, which broke constantly. I was terrified that she would put her hand in it, so we had it disconnected. Oh God, there were so many things.

Mother spent a lot of time rummaging around in drawers and boxes and she would spend a lot of time making packages. My clothes would disappear, my jewelry would disappear. The two of us were like two rats — she was wrapping things up and hiding them, and I was running around trying to find them. I was never afraid that she would set fire to the house or anything, I was just afraid that she would put away things and I'd never see them again. I didn't take mother out with friends, except for Edith and Susan. Edith and I were very close, as were Susan and I. They were just like family. Sometimes, such as Thanksgiving, I would have a few good friends here. There was no problem when I went out for an evening or when I entertained, which I didn't do very much. If I went out, I would pay someone to sit with her; when I entertained, mother would generally stay with the company. She would socialize with us through the cocktail hour. A lot of the people knew her. If she didn't recognize them she would talk and try to help out a little bit. She would somehow know that they were my guests. I think she had a feeling that she didn't want to intrude. She was quite sensitive about that. She did know that it was perhaps not appropriate for her to be there. Her sweetness was that she made it easy. She was very gracious. She didn't make anyone feel uncomfortable about her being there or about her leaving. So she would say goodnight and go upstairs. She would either read or go to bed.

What some of my friends would do from time to time was come and pick up mother and take her someplace for lunch — just to give me a break. Susan would come over and have coffee with her, but that was more for me than for my mother — to give me a couple of hours' break.

I think what made the situation so horrible was the feelings it evoked in me. Murderous rage, really — and such enveloping sadness — to want to kill and to want to weep at the same time. That went on and on and on. I went through a period of time — more at the beginning, I think — of having old feelings reawakened. There was a sort of gleeful maliciousness in some of my reactions to her, particularly in terms of my being more competent than she was. It was the first time in my life that I ever felt that way. All my life, my mother was "in charge." And I always had to struggle, somehow, to find my place in the sun. As bad as it was, there was something about this situation that at times I secretly relished.

These feelings were in the same category as the fantasies I had as a child. I would see myself lying in my coffin — the most beautiful corpse in the world — and my parents would be wringing their hands and howling with sorrow. "We are so sorry we were so mean to you." Of course, I was old enough to realize that it wouldn't be that good, because I wouldn't be alive to have the pleasure of seeing them feel so regretful.

My feelings at the time my mother was first with me were almost at this same age level. Although I wanted to, I couldn't say to her, "See, I'm really better than you are." I'm not as incompetent as you used to think I was. That was a lot of emotional baggage that I was carrying around and trying to deal with.

Akin to these feelings was the feeling that my mother had never appreciated me, as much as I felt I should have been appreciated. My brother was the favorite. I thought the situation was very ironic. Who was taking care of mother at this point? Not her favorite child. Not the one that was brilliant and marvelous — but the second-best child. This, of course, caused me to feel some anger at my brother, as well as some resentment of my mother. But it was a hollow kind of resentment. It's also a frustrating kind of resentment, because she wasn't there to understand. I couldn't get back at her. I couldn't say, "Look, isn't this ironic that I was the one that was the least favored, and now I'm the one taking care of you," and have her respond in a meaningful way.

When mother was first with me, she would get up in the middle of the night and go wandering around the house. I would get up in the middle of the night, and, every once in a while, I would find that she had wet her bed. At that time, she knew enough to be very humiliated, so she had to keep it from me. I couldn't know about that, so she would change her own linen. During this period, I spent a lot of time reassuring her about the things that went wrong. She was still intact enough to know that things were not well with her.

Mother would get dreadfully upset. Sometimes she had these horribly raging fits about what was happening to her — to the point where she would literally bang her head against the wall. "There's something the matter, there's something the matter." I think it was at that time I spoke to a psychiatrist, who then saw her for a while. He didn't give mother any medication, but he helped her. When things were getting to the point where I felt unable to leave her during the day, I got a housekeeper. My mother hated her. So I got another housekeeper and mother hated her, too, which was unusual, because my mother liked people. I think she hated the housekeepers

because of who they were. They were her sitters, and she knew
that they were there to supervise her. I tried very hard to get
the kind of person who would do what my father had done and
what I did — sort of pick up the pieces behind her and allow
her to do what she could for herself — the kind of person who
would help mother keep her pride and her self-esteem as much
as possible. These women were kind and they were good, but
they were not sensitive in that way, so they tended to patronize
her. And she didn't like it.

Things continued to get worse and worse. More and more,
mother did not want these women around. Also, the second
housekeeper began to be problematic herself. She had a child,
and she would want to bring her child with her. Sometimes she
did and sometimes she didn't. Sometimes she would show up
and sometimes she wouldn't. I was working and everything
was a mess. It was getting more and more difficult to hold
things together. I had gone through a horrible period before I
got the first housekeeper. I was into self pity. At the time, I
couldn't think of anything except quitting my job, staying
home, and martyring myself. I used to do a lot of raging
around. My reaction to her, and my feeling about her, at the
time, was the same as those I had toward my own children
when they were too young to be responsible for what they did.
The baby keeps you up all night long, crying, whining, and
clanging, but you don't let loose. You don't scream at the baby.
I couldn't scream at her, because I knew that she was totally incapable of knowing what she was doing.

It was like seeing some very beautiful piece of art being attacked by some kind of pollution — eroded and pitted and
faded. You get angry at what's happening, but you experience
a sadness, and such pity and compassion.

My mother's psychiatrist was pushing Oxford Home. He
was urging me to consider it. And I got to the point where I
thought, "If I am going to do it, I had better do it, while she
still has enough wits to be able to use the place in some appropriate way." I should have gotten her in there sooner than I did,

although she did go to day care there for a while. At Oxford, she started off on the ambulatory floor. I think she lasted on that floor for a couple of weeks — no more than two or three weeks. There wasn't enough supervision. There wasn't enough structure.

As I was going through all of this, I think one of the things that was most difficult was how hard it was to get support and understanding from members of the family and even from friends. My very closest friends — those people who were here a lot — saw exactly what was going on. So they would empathize. Those that did not, those that would see her out on the street in her $400 suit, with the beautiful hair, couldn't believe that she was as bad off as she was. Mother would put up a facade that could hold for a few social minutes, but people didn't realize that. She would say, "Oh, and how are you?" When she met you, she would avoid using your name, because she didn't know it. But she would know enough, to avoid it. "How are you and how is your family?" It sounds good. . . . She would confabulate like mad. She didn't know it, but you wouldn't know that she didn't. And so the neighbors and others who didn't know her that well would think, "She's terrific. She's fine. What's the matter with her daughter?" One of mother's sisters who visited here couldn't believe that there was something the matter with her. "Oh, she's just a little forgetful; aren't we all?" At the time she was wetting the bed. "She looks terrific!"

Mother would do so many things that seemed okay that the other things she did were hard to believe. And people didn't want to believe them anyway. So I'd get letters and calls from my cousins and aunts, saying, "All she needs is . . . ." "Why don't you . . . ?" I used to get so infuriated. What I was hearing was, "You have no reason to have any problem." And if I said, "Yes, there is a problem," it was as though I was saying something bad. It was a criticism of her and I shouldn't do that. Years later, when I was talking to one of her sisters — mother was in Oxford Home at the time — her sister said,

"Gee, she went so fast." To which I said, "What are you talking about? This has been going on since 1968. You just didn't want to believe it." When mother could still walk around, she could walk from here to Oak Hill Avenue, where I have a cousin, and back. She could do that even when she was terribly confused and mixed up. Then I would get a call at work from my cousin's wife, who is a nurse. She would say, "I just want you to know that your mother showed up here. She can stay for dinner." Or "We'll keep her here until you pick her up. Why don't you stop by for dinner?" Ellen saw it. At least she could see what was going on.

How did I manage through all of this? I was in therapy at the time. I was having a fair amount of it, and I am damned glad that I was.

Of course, when mother got to Oxford, she liked it — that is, when she learned her way around. I think mother was able to get used to the very different surroundings because she was not that aware of them. Perhaps, though, that is less true than the fact that my mother was not a materialistic woman — strangely enough. She had money to buy what she wanted . . . so that's what she bought. But she was not materialistic in a very strong sense of the word. Mother never complained — I don't ever remember my mother complaining. What she didn't like, I think she tried to change. But griping, complaining, moaning, whining — never. She was not the typical Jewish mother in that sense. She was a little too subtle.

Everything was easy for mother — or she tried to make you believe that. And nothing was too much for her to do for others. She was a very giving person. So I think that, when she found herself at Oxford, she must have decided to make the best of it. I felt sorry for her, but when I came to visit — until the very end when things were very bad with her — she seemed to be getting so much out of the fact that when she walked down the hall, people would say, "Hi, Ann." That was much more important to her, I think, than her surroundings.

Strangely enough — and I don't know how irrational this

sounds — I always thought, and I still think, that if Oxford Home had had the physical plant Lober House has now — I don't mean the set-up, but the physical plant — I would have thought of putting mother in Oxford practically from the beginning. Then she would have been going into a place that was more commensurate with what her lifestyle had been. I think Oxford would have been more acceptable to her and to me. Mother hadn't insisted on living with me. When I had talked about going to the Riverside Retirement Home or to one of the retirement hotels around here, she was not against the idea. So we went and looked at them. If Oxford had looked like a decent looking place, we probably would have considered it earlier. She would have gone to day care earlier and would have gotten in there much earlier. Knowing what her standards were, I don't think she would have accepted it at the time. She would not have accepted a place where she would have to walk down the hall to go to the toilet she would be sharing with several other women. In the late twentieth century, you just don't put people into boxes without toilets. If you have to go to the bathroom in the middle of the night, you need some privacy. I think going down the hall to the bathroom is dreadful. . . . Such a basic, fundamental right that people have — to be able to go into the toilet and close the door. And they didn't have that at Oxford.

It would also have been difficult for her to live in a room the size of those at Oxford. My kids went away to college and their dorm rooms were much bigger than the rooms at Oxford. Sharing a room was not a big deal. That would have been okay if it had been a large and attractively furnished room.

Where mother is now, at St. Elizabeth's, the physical plant is okay. It's clean and it's nice, and she does have a bathroom. But she's so incontinent that she doesn't even use the bathroom. She's getting perfectly good care and, in some respects, I think the nursing staff is better than the staff at Oxford. She's kept much cleaner. I have never approached her when she was incontinent. I have never approached her and leaned over to kiss her when she smelled of urine. She has no rashes or sores, so they're keeping her clean.

The pain in visiting her now is because of her condition, not because of her surroundings. I don't spend very long there. I stay an hour at most, and frequently it's less. I walk her around. We walk up and down the hall and wander around and if the weather is nice we go out and walk around the grounds for a while. I talk to her. Sometimes I sit and talk to her, but nothing I say sticks with her.

What is changed is that she used to read me a little bit. She does now, too, but even that's fading. I have to constantly remind her that I'm sitting with her. She gets distracted and looks away. She'll walk away from me. She's not connected at all. So when I'm sitting and talking to her, she is paying no attention to the words that are being said. She responds more to touch. If I hold her hand and stroke her, she'll respond, and she'll do that back. Sometimes, when I was leaving I would kiss her and she would kiss me back. She doesn't do that any longer. She doesn't recognize me as her daughter. And if I'm visiting her and I go out of the room and come back, she doesn't remember me. I don't know what goes on inside of her. I used to think that I would see a flash of recognition in her eyes, which would come and go very quickly. But I haven't even seen that in a while.

I try to get there once a week, but I don't always make it. There are times when I simply cannot get there. I dread the visits. It's just not the sort of thing that I get used to. When I worked at Oxford Home I used to see the families come — some of them were there all of the time. And at this nursing home, I see people that I know are there all the time. But I don't seem to be able to get used to what I'm going to see. I have to steel myself each time I go, and then when I leave. I leave with such a sense of relief. Oh, it's such a downer.

I have to get away from there, because being with her is so

emotionally debilitating.. Then it's with me on the drive home. You know, it's funny there's another thing that I've noticed since last winter. I find myself slipping, and talking about her as if she's dead. I have a feeling that if, in another six months, someone says to me, something about my parents, I could slip and say, "I don't have any. My parents are dead." I'm so close to feeling that way with her. With this kind of deterioration, with this kind of senility, the person is actually gone. There is no ego, there is no self. There is nothing. I could deal with some-one who is strapped in a wheelchair and couldn't move because she was so physically incapacitated, but whose mind was there. There would be someone who could relate to you. With my mother, it is just the opposite. Her body is still in good shape. Of course, she's not the way she used to be. She's much frailer and weaker, but, basically her physical health is good. She doesn't get sick. Her body is fine. But she's not the person she used to be. There really isn't a person there. So I keep holding on to what was — what was a long time ago — and that's where the sense that my mother's dead comes from.

I settled on visiting once a week, because it was what I could manage. I can go one week, two weeks, three weeks, and then I find that I can't manage it. But if I don't go two weeks in a row, I feel very guilty. And then I have to explain myself the next time I come. I visit on a weekend. It's an hour up and an hour back — that's two hours. And I'm so pressed for time, be-cause my weekends are so frequently rat races. I'm working full time, so on weekends I have to go the cleaners, go to the bank, to market, etc. You know how it is, you try and wash your floors and do your clothes and pay the bills, and on top of it, you've brought home work from the office that you've gotta do. The weekends are very very tight. If you want to meet a friend for lunch, or if you want to go out for an evening, or if you want to have some people in, it's very very difficult.

In terms of my life, I don't have time to go there to visit. I didn't feel that way when she went to Oxford, because when she first went there I got a greeting from her when I walked in. She knew me. I used to take her out. Many times that was the best way for me to visit with her, and she would like that. I didn't take her back home for a while, because I was afraid that it would be hard on her, that she wouldn't want to leave, that when I brought her here she would think that she was staying. But that didn't happen. When I saw that it didn't happen, I would bring her home and fix coffee for us. That was fine. I never had her stay overnight. It was easier for me to visit at Oxford Home, because I knew a lot of people, both residents and staff. It wasn't so bad.

The place she's in now — St. Elizabeth's — is different. I don't like it. I don't like the staff. They tend to be much less creative and more rigid than Oxford Home about how they deal with the residents. For instance, one day my mother wandered into the snack shop at St. Elizabeth's, turned on all the gas jets on the stove, and went away. The staff's answer was to restrain her. I called my mother's psychiatrist and said, I'm appalled, I can't stand it. So we had some meetings with their staff and we talked about the problem. What the staff came up with was that they would do everything they could to get a volunteer to accompany her wherever she went. For the staff to make that room or the kitchen part of it unavailable to her was not feasible, they said. It was feasible. They could have put a cover over the knobs of the range. Their way of dealing with wanderers or whatever, is to restrain them. They run the home by protecting the residents from each other in this fashion. So if I told them I would rather have her up and walking around than tied in a chair — even though she might fall and break a hip — I would be a rotten daughter.

I don't want to get involved with the staff and become very involved with the day-to-day care of my mother. I don't want that. I feel somewhat bad about this. I wish that feeling this was okay — that it was really acceptable. I know it's not. So, to that extent, I feel badly.

They have a good staff up at that nursing home. They have a good social worker there, but she doesn't know what its all about. Most of the people the staff see — most of the children they see — are over invested, overactive. But the staff sees that as the norm. And I remember that we did too when I was working at Oxford Home. That's the right way, that's the healthy way, that's the good way. I think the staff at Oxford Home was probably a little more open to understanding the middle generation. But I don't think that most people really are. I wonder what it would have been like for her and for me if I had been working there when she came in. But by the time she was admitted there I had been gone from Oxford for a few years. I notice now that when I'm dealing professionally with that group of people — particularly daughters — I am able to relate and to understand them in a way I never did before. I think that I bring an added dimension to my work with people in that situation. I feel I can be empathetic as to what it is like to live with a mentally deteriorating parent or to have to visit such a parent in an institution. It's the kind of thing that, unless you've been through it, you don't appreciate what it's like to be with someone without intellectual awareness. It's such a wrenching kind of experience.

In many ways, what makes it so very different is that people don't talk about it very much and, if they do, they aren't honest about it. When Lou died, I felt a lot of support and understanding for my feelings, an understanding that I don't feel with my mother's situation. There's something different. It's a hidden thing. It's like years ago, people didn't talk about incest for example. And there's still something almost taboo about being honest how one feels about such an experience.

There have been times when I wished with all my heart that the phone would ring and they would tell me that my mother had died. That would be a blessing. When I saw the beginning of her deterioration, I wished that she would have a heart attack and die, because I knew what was down the road.

I wish that the staff at this nursing home, for instance, would be able to understand, so that I would not have to feel so goddamn guilty if I missed a weekly visit. I think this feeling comes from both of us — me and the staff. I feel guilty and they reinforce it. They don't say anything openly, but there are subtle little ways that they get it across. "Oh, I haven't seen you, Mrs. Goldman. We missed you." That's all it takes. Or, "Your mother needs some hose and we really didn't know what to do about it." Implied, of course, if I had been there every day I would have known that she needed them. She has money there, I don't know why somebody couldn't go out and buy her a pair of stockings. Sometimes I think that they are not even aware of the message that they've been giving.

When all of this was first happening, my children were still in Chicago. Actually, Michael was pushing for some kind of nursing home long before I was — despite the fact that he cared a good deal for her. He cared a lot, but he was worried about me. That was some time after my husband died. I looked lousy at the time, and Michael was worried. He used to spend a lot time trying to talk me into doing something like putting her into Oxford. I had my children's support — no question about that. Daniel was in graduate school far away, and I really don't know how he felt about it. Maybe a little less adamant than Michael for the placement. But he never said anything, since he wasn't here and didn't see her. His attitude was it had to be my decision. I was the one who had to live with the current situation and live with whatever my ultimate decision was. Although he didn't try to advise me, there was no question that I had his full support in whatever I decided.

Daniel was home one time for a vacation, when my mother was in her middle phase so to speak. He was marvelous with her. He was absolutely marvelous. They baked bread together, and she was thrilled. He did a lot of creative things with her. He never patronized her. He never talked down to her, which is easy to do under the circumstance. Of course he was only here for about two weeks. That makes a big difference.

Michael and Daniel and I haven't talked about it, but I would be very surprised if they had not thought about my situation when I get older. I think about it too, and I worry about it. I don't think that they worry, but I do. I'm scared, because I think that there are some genetic components of this condition. So of course every time I forget something — and I do forget — I think what's going to happen? I have visions of myself in mother's condition. Maybe that's one of the reasons it's so painful for me to be with my mother. I see myself there. It's just overwhelming. It's times like that when I really do believe it would be nice if we could work out some system when, at a given point, a committee or somebody says, "Here drink this, Honey." And that's the end of that.

You know, I think to myself, "That's what I'll do. I'll take care of it. When I begin to get bad I'll find a bottle of pills and that will be that." Of course I know that everybody has thought that, but they don't do it. So, I realize that I won't do it either, which makes it even worse. You don't know it until it's so far gone you can't do anything.

If I could I'd like to give a message to people in general. And that message is to not judge children in terms of the way they take care of their parents. You can't do that. You have no right to judge unless you've really been there. It's the same as judging those who have been faced with pulling the plug on another human being. You can't judge people who are in that kind of situation. You have no right to. You don't really know what the chidlren are struggling with or what it was like for them.

It would have been very nice for me and my mother if there had been a really good day care facility where I could have dropped her off in the morning — a place where she would have had her meals and some social activities. A place where she would be cared for through the day and where she could stay if I wanted to go away for a week's vacation or whatever. It would have been so nice if she could have been in some kind of facility where she would have care during the day and where I wouldn't be afraid every time the phone rang at work that I would have to drop everything and come home.

Even though I'm a professional, it was very difficult for me to work out something for my own mother. I had very few choices. And if we hadn't had money, there would have been even fewer choices. I was fortunate, because I could hire a homemaker. I could send her off to camp. I could send her off to a psychiatrist. I had some choices — not very many — the fact that we weren't poor was a help. People who are poor are even more limited.

One of the more frustrating things is that if you are the child, other people don't listen to you. Your opinion is somehow seen as being distorted — for whatever reason. It's not taken seriously. That's the reaction I got from my family. And that's the reaction I got from doctors. I think it's pervasive among professionals that when somebody — closely related, but not professional — offers them observations or opinions, professionals tend to disregard it. The mother who brings her child to the pediatrician is frequently treated like an hysterical mother and her observations are ignored. It's that sort of attitude that I think many professionals have. Persons who are closest to a situation — and really should be paid attention to — are very frequently depreciated.

My mother took a real turn for the worse when she was moved out of Oxford Home. She was told that the home was closing, but she couldn't understand what that was all about. As it turned out, the timing of the move was very bad, because I was out of town, giving a paper in San Francisco. I didn't move her. And want to know something? I was not sorry that I was away.

At this point after several years in St. Elizabeth's, mother is very very regressed. She is unable to speak, and she hasn't been able to feed herself for several years now. She has no mechanism for letting anyone know what she wants, or even whether she's in pain. Mother spends most of the time lying in bed dozing. At times, its hard to know if she's even conscious. If she does happen to be sitting in a chair, very soon her head will droop and she'll doze off again.

The nurses walk her as much as possible, so she doesn't develop any sores. I walk her, too. But for all intents and purposes, she is helpless, as helpless as a six-day-old infant. Hardly anything stimulates her — although she will, sporadically, respond to touching. If she were left alone, she would die. Clearly she has moved more and more to the end position where all awareness is gone and everything has shut down.

To visit her now is very difficult. While, at one time, I would try carrying on a conversation as though she had answered. I would say "I heard from your sister Sadie. Yes, she's feeling fine." But now she doesn't comprehend anything. She's totally not there. She doesn't make eye contact. There is nothing. I'm still visiting at the same rate, but I don't know why. It's not something that you think about. I'm not all that compulsive about being there every single week. There are times when a week will go by, or two weeks, and I don't get there. One of the reasons for going there, of course is to make sure that the staff continues to take care of her — although I know very well they are. And I suppose another reason I go is to see if she needs anything, although I can't imagine what. She's not even getting dressed, so I don't need to be there to see that she has shoes or a new blouse. I don't really know why I go. She's my mother. I'm her daughter. She has no one else, and I'm there.

It's a long drive to St Elizabeth's. I suppose that, over the winter, if the weather is bad on a bitter, cold, icy Saturday or Sunday, I won't go. I wish I could say that I feel comfortable about not going. I do call from time to time. Somehow it just doesn't seem the same. I wish I didn't feel so compelled to visit her. I do it out of a sense of guilt and obligation and duty.

Somewhere it is programed into me that this is what a good daughter would do. Not to visit means I'm not being a good daughter. And I suppose the bottom line, in the end, is that it's easier for me to go than to deal with my feelings about not going. It's like the lesser of two evils.

I think it would be easier for me not to go if someone on that staff would say to me, "You know this is ridiculous. You chase yourself up here. There's no need. We are taking good care of her. She doesn't know whether you're here or not. If we need you, or if we think you should be here, we would let you know." I would like them to give me permission not to go. But they never do that. Nobody has said that to me. If they said that, I think I would feel comfortable if I got there every month, or five or six weeks. I would not feel that if I were at home or doing something else that that becomes sort of tainted by the fact that I should be there. As a professional in the field, I would have said that to a family member in my situation, but I can not say it to myself. You know, if the social worker or the nurse said that to me, that would do it for me. But I can't give permission to myself.

I think that it wouldn't take much more than the other "parent" (St. Elizabeth House) to say, "Enough, you don't have to do that. It's not helping. It's not necessary. It's a waste." All the things that I say to myself. But I feel that my not being there is interpreted as I don't give a damn. Staff might feel that if the daughter doesn't care why should they? Or they could feel "Poor soul. She doesn't have a daughter who will come and take care of her, so I will." I know, from my years at Oxford, that the staff becomes so very invested and, sometimes, overly invested, so that if they're pouring themselves into caring for a resident, then they get very angry if the next of kin is not as invested. It gets very complicated.

I think another piece of why I go is that I know my mother. I know that, if it were the other way around she would be doing it. When I was a child, I almost died. Mother evidently nursed me night and day for weeks on end — and then would get up early in the morning. My parents took a cottage at the sea shore, simply because they thought the salt air would be good for me. When I would have coughing spells, mother would wake up at 5:00 A.M. and take me down to the beach. She would sit with me hour after hour after hour. I was an infant; I didn't experience it. My fantasy is that if things were now reversed, and if I were ill and helpless, she would be sitting at my side. There's a lot of difference. With me, there was something that could be done, and there was a life to be lead. With her, there is nothing. There's no life ahead of her. There's nothing that can be done to save her. But, somehow, all the cognitive stuff doesn't seem to be quite as powerful as the emotional kinds of issues that get stirred up.

That's what keeps coming back. The resentment and the hurt have long since been swept away. They seem less important. They become petty. I think we all, somewhere along the line, forgive our parents. See them as fallible. Forgive them for some of the hurts, or the misunderstandings, or the lack of empathy that we've experienced. Now when the parent is at the end of life other things become more important. I guess that is where the guiltiness comes in. I'm not doing as well by her as she did by me. When my mother first went to Oxford Home, there was a time when I would hear people talking about a parent who was aging or not doing well. They would be talking about someone's son or daughter (usually the daughter), saying, "Oh she would never put her mother in a nursing home. She keeps her at home. She does 'xyz' for her." I would hear that and it would feel like a reproach to me. I knew very well I couldn't take care of her at home. Even if I weren't working, it wouldn't have been good to take care of her at home. I just didn't have the wherewithall to do that.

While I don't like the uncreative way the staff at St. Elizabeth's solves problems with patients, and while I don't like the guilt trip they lay on me — intentionally or unintentionally, or that I'm laying on me — what choice do I really have? Since I can't take care of my mother at home, the only thing I could say to the people at St. Elizabeth's is, "That's it, I'll take her elsewhere." But I know, if I take her elsewhere, I'll just find the same thing over and over and over again.

A GIFT FROM THEM

In the midst of a network of former students, Jane Stanhope helped to care for two famous, but aging ballet dancers during the last year of their lives — lives that ended within three weeks of each other. A former student and prima ballerina herself, Jane shared caring responsibilities with more than a dozen other former students. Each brought the gift of his own particular talent or skill — a lawyer, an accountant, a symphony cellist.

Whether they were cooking dinner, writing checks, hiring nurses, or playing music for them, this special group enriched the last months of Royce's and Martin's lives, blunting much of the pain and suffering with love and caring concern.

Royce and Martin — these two elderly gentlemen were my teachers. They were my ballet teachers. I've known them since I was about 11 years old and they were in their middle thirties. They seemed to me, at that time, like two fathers. My own father, who was very athletic, liked them and approved of my ballet training. Later on, I danced with both of them, so they then were my associates. And all through my career they were my mentors. I made a good career in ballet and they were proud of me.

As the years went on, I would see Royce and Martin several times a year — I would take them out for dinner or they would take me out for dinner. In daughterly fashion, I would sit and listen to them as they chattered on and on about themselves and their students. In their later years, when they became more frail, I became closer to them than I had been as a child. Actually, the relationship was now on a different level. I became their friend. They had many, many friends. They had no family in the city, but they had many friends.

They finally reached the point where those of us who were

close friends could see that they were beginning to show the signs of old age. Even so, they were still teaching at their studio. Martin developed cancer. He had to have several operations, but he continued to teach. It had come to the point, though, where neither of them could dance in their class anymore. They had to walk around and stand and teach. Then Royce had a slight stroke. Afterwards, he found that he would lose his balance, so he had to sit and teach. And that was very, very frustrating for him because he had been a top classical ballet dancer, and enjoyed demonstrating so much.

As these definite signs of age appeared, the two of them realized that they were going to have to give up their studio. I was one of the people involved in giving them a "closing party." Some 600 to 800 people came in from all over the country for the party. Royce and Martin were surprised. They didn't know they had so many friends. And, of course, all of these people who came to the closing party put them in the best of spirits. They closed the studio that summer, but they were still in good spirits.

Just before they closed their own studio, they were invited to teach at another studio, because they were very famous. The weather was cold that winter and it was hard for Royce and Martin to get to the studio. I drove them down a few times, but they were finding that they could hardly teach. In fact, they had students teaching for them. Often they couldn't make it to the studio for one reason or another, but they still persevered and began their second year cheered on by their loyal students. Martin was 79 by then. It was just too much for them. In December, they realized that they had taken one step too far.

The following May, Royce had a massive stroke and was in the Rehabilitation Institute for four months. During that time, he had to learn everything over. He had to learn to speak, to write, to move — everything from A to Z. Martin, of course, wasn't well either. He had had a number of operations. As I had said, I didn't know until the end just how severe they were. He was riddled with cancer. But he had an indomitable will. So he kept going on and on.

Royce and Martin had lived in a third-floor walk-up apartment. It had no air conditioning. They actually lived in side-by-side, mirror-image apartments with high ceilings and a skylight. Each had one enormous room — probably 30' × 25'. And each had a tiny little kitchen — just a corner of a kitchen. They used Martin's little sink to wash their face and hands. And they used Royce's kitchen for cooking. (Royce loved to cook.) Out in the hall there was a toilet and down the hall was a shower. It was not too far from their studio. And that's where they lived for forty years.

Every August before that final summer, the two of them had taken off for Europe or for some place else. Well, that last August, Martin was alone in the apartment, because Royce was in Rehab. He was in that apartment every day. That was the year that we had 47 days of over 90-degree temperature. And their apartment was at least 10 degrees hotter than it was outside. During all of this, Martin never complained. Since Martin was alone, groups of us would take him out to lunch or take him out to dinner.

Sometime during that summer, Martin finally agreed that they should move. (In fact, he had wanted to move for some time.) Well, Royce and Martin had moved into that place in 1940, I think. And, oh, the accumulation of things! It was unbelievable how much stuff they had — very nice things. . . . Once Martin made the decision to move, a group of us decided to help move them. He had found an apartment over on North Lake Drive. It was just two small rooms, but it had a bathroom *in* the apartment and a *real* kitchen — all that luxury. It also had air conditioning, which of course they had never had before. But they would never use it, as it turned out. There were five of us who moved them in 90-degree heat.

Martin was a very clever man, I will say that. He had so

many friends. And he knew how to use friends, because in the years of owning the ballet studio, he had had to manage all sorts of performances on volunteer help. So he put someone in charge of moving all of the kitchen and someone in charge of moving all of the bathroom things and someone in charge of all the books and someone in charge of this and someone in charge of that. To tell you how many books they had, the appraiser has just finished cataloging them, and the catalog is two inches thick.

The day of the move — after the mover had left — I went over to pick up Martin and take him home to dinner. He was exhausted. Royce, of course, was still in the Rehab Institute. When I walked into the apartment, furniture and books were everywhere. I said, "Martin, have the movers finished?" He said, "Yes, they're finished. I just have a few things left." I thought, "My God, a few things! It's another four-hour move." Then I thought, "What *is* he *thinking*?" So I said, "Do you want to come home with me tonight?" "Oh no, that's all right. That's all right. I'll just look to see what I have to do." Well, he should have come, because he collapsed in the heat and he broke his leg very badly. He was already in bad shape because of the cancer. Martin wound up in the hospital — this was in August — and he stayed there until just before Thanksgiving, just healing the leg.

The group, of course, arranged to have the rest of their things moved into the new apartment. One of the gals in the group was an interior decorator and she did her best, arranging things and making the apartment as comfortable as possible. Martin and Royce hadn't moved in 40 years. They had accumulated all of those things and they never moved them. They had no idea what moving was all about. I've moved 16 times in my life, and "move" is a four-letter word!

Soon after we had everything moved in, Royce arrived, and he was raring to go. He had come out of Rehab using a walker. He had learned how to speak again and he had learned how to yell at everybody again. From the time he moved into the apartment, Royce started issuing commands. He had been in the army — a master sergeant and he was issuing commands as usual. You would no more open the door but he was yelling at you to do something. "Bring it here." "All right, Royce, here it is," "Well, set it down. Not over there! Over here." He was having a little difficulty with his speech, but he managed.

Every day Royce had to do his exercises, so he would go out into the hallway, go all the way down the hall and back again on his walker. One time, when he got down to the end of the hall, he became dizzy. He was afraid and he didn't know quite what to do. So he knocked on a door. Someone was there, fortunately, and the lady helped him back to his apartment. I think, though, that the incident made him very much afraid.

One day, my ten-year-old son and I took Royce out to Mc-Donald's. When we went into the McDonald's not too far from the apartment, we made some special arrangements with a young man there, in case Royce might want to take a cab and go down there on his own. The young man at McDonald's was going to help him with a hamburger, which he liked, and help him get a cab back home. That would give Royce a nice sort of independence. But I don't think he went out much after that. He may have gone out one or two times, but I'm not sure.

I have a feeling that he had a lot of fear inside him. Also, a lot of pride. He was a very handsome man — tall and handsome. And I think he was afraid of falling down or doing something that would have embarrassed him. I think his fear and his pride sort of slowed him down. I also think that he felt his life had become very sad — having to remain inside and not being able to get around.

Then Martin came home. Martin was in very sad shape. He was wearing a cast on his leg. He had lost a tremendous amount of weight and his face was so haggard. Royce would look at Martin and it took something out of him. As time went on, Martin began looking . . . disheveled. The nurses just could not keep him as neat and clean as he was used to. How could they get him in and out of the tub with that cast on?

There was another problem on Martin's return. The two men had lived for 40 some years, side-by-side in two separate apartments. When they closed their doors, they had had their privacy. Then all of a sudden, these two men were living in the same small apartment. There were many adjustments to be made. Things were not the way they wanted them and Royce, in particular, was so frustrated because he could not make them the way he would like. For one thing, Royce was a very clean person. And even though they had good nurses, things were not as clean as Royce wanted. Royce despised not having things as he liked them.

Martin, on the other hand, was a different kind of person. He loved life and anything in it. Anything that came along, Martin could handle. He went along with everything. He had been toughened growing up in Montana, for instance, experiencing the rigors of a forty below winter.

In other ways, they were different, too. Martin wanted to see people. Royce couldn't care less. He had a therapist from Rehab come in to see him a couple of times a week. He had all sorts of exercises to do. He also had speech lessons. Royce had a definite schedule and he was a creature of habit. He did all of these exercises in the morning and right after lunch, off he would go to take his little nap. Then he would get up and was ready to face his world. At that time, he seemed like a spoiled child, only interested in himself. On the other hand, Martin looked forward to seeing people.

So now let me tell you about the parade of people who came to visit and care for them. We had one young man, for example, who had been a student of theirs. He would come every week and spray all of the plants because, of course, Royce and Martin had brough their forest with them when they moved.

There was a lady who lived down the street a block away who came in almost every morning, just to say "Good morning," and to see if everything was all right. Then, about four blocks away, there was another woman who would come in about once a week.

There was a young woman attorney who was a good friend of theirs. She had also been a student. Shelly helped them hire the nurses and generally watched over the two men. Royce and Martin had an accountant, another student, who would come in every Sunday. She would do their bills and anything else that needed doing. Martin tried to do these things, because he was the bookkeeper of the two, but he was so weak that he just couldn't. At the end — from November on — Martin could hardly even write his name, he was so weak.

I would come over once a week and cook dinner. One of the problems was that the nurses really didn't know how to cook the kind of dinner that Royce and Martin liked. When I came, I would cook a nice dinner for us. Then we would sit down to eat and pretend to be out in some very special place. In a sense, it was like old times. They liked that very much. There was another former student who came — a cellist from the Chicago Symphony Orchestra. When she came, she brought her cello and played for them.

There were about 15 people coming in on a regular basis. Each one would do some little thing — go to the store, bring a pie. I'd always bring something I had made. These were very special people. All of them had been related, in some way, to Royce and Martin in the past. The only new relationships were the round-the-clock nurses. It was an extraordinary situation. Royce and Martin were very lucky. Others in a similar situation are not so cared for.

Martin, however, was very unhappy up until Christmas. Then he began to receive a lot of Christmas cards and calls. Martin became concerned that people didn't know how ill they were. So after Christmas, I wrote a kind of follow-up Christ-

mas letter. He wrote it, actually. It was the last thing he wrote
in his own handwriting. I had it mimeographed and sent out
about 200 copies. All through the years, Martin had edited a
letter, which he sent out whenever he felt like it — about five to
ten times a year. It was called "The Loft News" and it had to do
with dance history and all the chatty gossip around the studio.
As a result, he had, over the years, kept in contact with about
600 people. Martin was, by far, the more gregarious of the
two. I don't mean as far as being a talker. Royce was the
talker; he wasn't the letter writer.

As soon as the letter went out, the response was incredible!
One person who received the letter would tell five others.
Pretty soon there was a stack of mail a mile high. People were
concerned. They were sending money and gifts. It was incredible. And all of this time, both of them were going steadily
down hill. After Christmas, steadily going down, down, down,
down.

Martin went into the hospital in January for a colostomy.
When he returned home, he was very weak. Then Royce developed a cough and, observing Martin's pathetic condition,
depressed him even more. Then one day, Royce said in a loud
voice — loud enough for the nurse to hear — "The medication
is very confusing. I don't understand it. They've changed it
and I don't understand it." And I thought, "That's strange!
That's really strange!" Royce never said that anything was
confusing. He was on top of everything his whole life.

About this time, Shelly, the attorney, said to me, "You
know, Jane, there's not much money left. I think we should get
them into a nursing home. It's costing a small fortune for these
nurses." And seeing Martin in my mind's eye, I thought, "My
God, that man is going to die any day." Royce was still walking
around, still depressed, but still walking around — at least if
someone helped him up to his walker. One of Royce's lungs
had been removed in the forties. In December, he had had
pneumonia and now he was couching again. So anyway,

Shelly said to me, "You're the one that's going to tell Martin. Jane, you have to do it. You're the only one they're going to listen to." Shelly was the person who had the final word in matters relating to Royce and Martin. So I just sort of went by what Shelly said. Even though she was younger than I, I felt that, since she was an attorney, she knew all of these things.

Early in the day, I sat down with Martin — because Martin was the one who was always in charge of everything — and I said, "Look, it's going to be really hard. We know and you know that it's going to be very soon and you'll be gone." Martin nodded, because he was ready. He was ready to die. And I said, "It's going to be very, very hard for us to take Royce to a nursing home, once you're gone." It took me two hours to have this conversation, because it was a very delicate conversation. Right now, I'm being blunt, but then it was a very, very quiet and careful conversation. Martin thought it over, and he said, "I guess you're right. I'll talk it over with Royce."

The very next morning, the lawyer called me and said, "Jane, let's forget it. We aren't going to do this. We're not going to put them in a nursing home." She said, "Call him back." I said, "Oh, thank God, Shelly. I just felt so terrible about saying that to him." So I called him up right away, and I got Royce on the phone. When I said, "Hello Royce," Royce said, "Oh, Jane, Martin isn't feeling so well." So I said, "Let me talk to him for just a minute." I talked to Martin, and I said, "Martin, please forget what we talked about yesterday. I'm so sorry. You just forget what we said. You are both going to stay there. Don't even think about it."

I found out later that Royce had a seizure about a half hour after I talked to Martin. He died in the hospital four days later. I asked the doctor what happened. "Do you know what caused it?" And he said it was some sort of chemical change to begin with, but it was pneumonia that caused his death. When the doctor said that, I thought, "Chemical change? Why chemical change?" Then I remembered what Royce had said about medication being confusing. I felt that my suspicions were right that Royce overdosed himself. The doctor will not agree with me, but that's how I felt. I don't know if Royce and Martin talked it over or not, but I have a feeling they did. And I feel he overdosed himself. I also have this horrible feeling of anger at myself. Why did I say anything at all to Martin? I have this feeling of guilt. I believe that I may have been the one who caused Royce's death.

On the other hand, I believe that Royce went the way he would have preferred to go. And I respect him for that. Knowing the kind of person Royce was, I think it would have been the greatest tragedy in the world for him to have gone to a nursing home — and be tied to a chair or restrained in any way.

After Royce died on February 10, Martin's whole body fell apart. Everything went wrong. I remember the last time I saw him at home. The nurse was holding a glass up for him — he didn't have any strength left at all. He sipped the liquid and then he looked at me. I thought he was going to say something *terribly* important. And he said, "I just *love* cranberry juice." He wouldn't complain about anything. Every single thing that happened to him, Martin could accept. That was the very last thing he ever said to me. At that time, he had a blockage of the bladder and he finally went to the hospital. After that, he was comatose. He died four days later on February 29. Had Martin been hanging on to be sure that Royce was okay? I think so. It seemed that way very often, because Martin was just like a living ghost.

I never asked the lawyer why she changed her mind about the nursing home. I think she might have called the doctor and the doctor might have said, "They are in such bad shape, don't do anything. They'll be gone soon." I really don't know. I never talked to Shelly about it. I felt that she was trying to do the best job that she could do. We all tried to do the best we could. I respected her judgement. We all make mistakes, and we can't live our lives walking on egg shells. I know she was very concerned about the money. The nurses were costing — are you ready for this — $6,000 per month. And Shelly was thinking that if Royce lasted two more years, there would be absolutely nothing left. Not too many people in this world have that kind of money. I worked at the apartment for about a month after their deaths, going through all of their things and seeing that people who needed to be contacted — the heirs and so on — were contacted. Royce and Martin had become very close to me, and I wanted to be involved. Martin had asked me earlier to be trustee for his will. If I hadn't been, I would have felt a great loss. It would have been like cutting an arm off. Because I was involved with their things, I got to know them even better. I saw the things they had and the kinds of things they appreciated. There was a side of them that I knew as a daughter figure, but going through their things, I saw another side — what kind of music they liked, the kinds of books they read, the various attitudes they had. I found out things about their families that I hadn't known. I found out about moneys they had loaned. They had given some money to Indians in Utah and I read the thank you letter they received. All of these things reaffirmed my belief that they were really very nice people.

Historically, I found it very interesting to read all of the things they had collected over many, many years. As a result of going through those things, I have been involved in seeing that these go to the right places — the historical society or the arts library. The families were not interested in them. They weren't totally disinterested, but they really didn't know Royce and Martin, and I don't think they would have known the significance of what they had left.

Royce and Martin were both famous, but in different ways. Royce was famous because he was a classical dancer, a kind of modern dancer, and a choreographer. He was an associate of Ruth Page, who was famous in her own right. Martin didn't start dancing until he was 24. He was a well-known clas-

sical dancer, but it was his studio that really made Martin. He
knew how to manage. In 40 years, the two of them had 30,000
students. And that's a lot of ballet students. They had world-
wide recognition.

After the two of them died, the newspaper writer that I'm
meeting for lunch today wrote a small article for the Post about
Martin. She gave the information to the Herald Tribune and
the Tribune printed an article about Royce. Other papers began to pick up the information. Then there was a four-column
article in the dance section of the New York Times that told
about Royce and Martin and their contributions to ballet. The
New York Times writer had unearthed a whole chapter of this
city's history — the chapter about when we had been the ballet
capital of the United States. If that writer had not done some
digging, we would be the poorer. It is because of the many people who were involved with Royce and Martin that we have a
history. We have something now for other people to build on.

In his will, Royce had asked to be cremated. And in his
will, Martin asked to be buried in his family plot. We arranged
all of those things. Royce died first and he was cremated. I
asked that nothing be done with his ashes until after Martin
died. When Martin died, we placed the urn with Royce's ashes
in Martin's casket and sent the casket to Montana. Some dis-
tant cousins out there had a small graveside service. They buried them together. That was their wish.

We had decided among ourselves — the group that was taking care of them — that we would have a memorial service
when they both were gone. And we decided that we would
send out a notice that there was going to be a service, doing it
long enough ahead so that anyone who wanted to come in
from out of town would have the time to do it. We sent the
notice to this long mailing list — the one I had gone through at
Christmas time.

Earlier, I had asked Martin if there was any kind of music
that he would like to have at a service. "Yes," he said, "the

Brahms Requiem." And I thought, "My God, a hundred singers and the Symphony Orchestra. How are we going to do this?" I think Martin was the more religious of the two. Royce did not want a service. He wanted to be cremated and that was all.

We tried to make the service as nice and sentimental as we could. We asked various people to speak. About eight of them did. Then one of the ladies who was on the board of the church were we had the service read from the Bible. The organist from a church in Twin Oaks, who had known them from the thirties and had written scores for many of their ballets, played excerpts from them and parts of the Brahms Requiem. The class accompanist played music they liked to use in class. We really tried. It was a celebration of life.

After the service, we had a get-together in the church's community room. It was like an alumni gathering. Later on, the insiders group had dinner at a restaurant right below their old studio, where they went every single day for lunch. The waitress at the restaurant had set two places for them. When we sat down, she said, "I know, I know what they want." Then she put a bottle of beer and a glass at one place and a glass of port wine at the other. Martin liked port wine and Royce liked beer. We really felt that Royce and Martin were there with us. It was a rousing dinner — lots of drinking, lots of laughing, and lots of recalling all sorts of funny situations. There was nothing somber about that dinner.

One gal (a former student of theirs and the person who began dance therapy in New York) wanted to plan a New York get together. So they had their own little memorial service the day before ours. I said "service" but it really turned out to be a cocktail party. We had arranged for them to call us during their get together which coincided with a gathering of the heirs and some of the helpers at Royce and Martin's apartment. They called us and said, "We're having a great time!"

The experience with Royce and Martin taught us the value

of esprit d' corps, or community spirit. When you are the only
one helping, it can seem very grim. When you are one of a
group constantly communicating with one another, you not
only make it easier but you also do a better job! And it even
can be fun. It was a very positive experience. It made me feel
like a much better person. And I'm sure everyone else would
have said the same thing. This was Royce and Martin's gift to
us.

3.

PUTTING IT ALL TOGETHER

YOU HAVE just read the very personal, often painful, stories of twelve men and women — the heros and heroines of this book — who, at varying stages of their own lives, faced and accepted responsibility for an older person. (In a very real sense, everyone in this situation is a hero or a heroine.)

The men and women in this book told you simply and openly about their lives, their relationships, and their feelings. Each person dealt with his situation in his own way, doing the best he could in terms of his own expectations of himself, in terms of society's expectations of him, and in terms of resources and knowledge at the time. Common threads of feelings run throughout these stories — love, hate, frustration, pity, guilt, anger, anxiety, dispair. These stories show that, however different the situations are, a common experience has been shared.

If you are going through a similar experience, know that, as you read these words, millions of other people are sharing your feelings, debating the same issues, and having the same worries about what the future holds for them. Others have already gone through it — have gone through it, have survived, and have grown through the experience.

If you have not yet been through this, you may want to think, in advance, about how you would cope if you found

209

yourself in such a situation. Almost certainly, you will find yourself involved — directly or indirectly — in the care of an older person, whether it is a family member or a friend. Answering the following questions may help you. Answer them honestly, discussing your responses with members of your family. Then use your responses — and theirs — as the basis for planning how you would face and resolve the dilemma of caring for an older loved one.

How Do I Really Feel About This Person? What Has Our Relationship Been Over the Years? What Is It Likely to be in the Future?

Before you answer this question, you might want to remind yourself that feelings are neither "good" nor "bad." They are the natural responses to people, situations, and events that are conditioned by your life experiences and by your interactions with that person from childhood on. It is healthy to openly recognize and acknowledge whatever feelings you have, so that even negative ones can be examined and faced without guilt. You don't have to love your mother or your grandmother just because she is your mother or grandmother. Try to understand that person, yes; but love her unconditionally, no. This is not necessary and, sometimes, not even appropriate. Try to give yourself permission to honestly accept your feelings. They exist. To pretend otherwise can be more costly, over time, than the painful acceptance of them in the beginning.

Partly because her mother did not raise her and partly because of the kind of person her mother was, Marty had very ambivalent feelings about her. Marty was bedeviled by the need to have her mother's love, as well as by the need to love her mother unequivocally. Because she was an only child, Marty felt the guilty need to take care of her mother — a need that colored her thoughts and actions, and affected her family life, even her marital relationship with her husband. Marty needed her mother to *truly* love her in a way that was meaningful to Marty. Her mother, however, may not have been capable of doing that.

Given their relationship and Pat Hughes's feelings about her mother, over the years, it would have been unrealistic and maybe even detrimental for Pat to have moved home to care for her mother. Pat had struggled, emotionally, so long and so hard, to become her own person.

Tom and his sisters loved their mother. And although there had been some strained relationships along the way, their decisions concerning their mother were made without inhibiting, strong, and conflictual emotions. On the other hand, Flo had had no relationship at all with her mother-in-law. In fact, she had met her husband's mother only once before she came to live with them. Both Tom and Flo had feelings about the situation, but, by and large, these feelings were manageable.

When you think how you feel about your loved one, think, too, about what your relationship with that person has been over the years. You may have a genuine love and respect for a parent or grandparent, but if that person's aloofness or autocratic style has resulted in a formal relationship between the two of you, could you live with him in close quarters for any extended period of time? What habits does this person have — particularly habits that may be difficult for you to live with. What about your habits and your family's habits? Are you able to make any reasonable adjustments that may be necessary? Allowing for these adjustments, can you live compatibly?

What Do I Feel Obligated to Do? Why Do I Feel That Way?

By definition, an obligation is an action imposed by law, society, or conscience. For some people, the obligation to care for an older person stems from conscience; for others, it stems from societal pressures — a strong, pervasive, and, for some, an inappropriate response to a situation. Acting solely on obligation may be a disservice not only to yourself, but also to your loved one. If you feel obligated, try to find out why you

feel that way. Then try to determine the validity of those feelings of obligation.

Martin felt obligated — both by a son's love of his parents
and by a pact he made with his sister — to see that his mother
and father lived out their lives in their own home, whatever it
took. Flo felt obligated to care for her mother-in-law, not only
out of love for her husband, but also because it became clear
that there would be no help from her husband's brother. With
Mae, it was the obligation felt because of the trouble she believed she had caused her mother when she was a child.

What Do I Really Want to Do?

Once you have recognized and examined your feelings
about the person, as well as your feelings of obligation, and, it
is hoped, come to terms with them, your mind will be freer to
focus on what you really want to do in caring for that older
person. Even these wants may need to be compromised, however.

Although she might have felt the obligation of an only
child, Carol really wanted to take care of her mother in her
home. For Jim and Jane, caring for the older person was solely
a matter of choice. There were no obligations on their part —
real or perceived — save that of friendship. Jane, as one of a
network of caring friends, was helping, truly, out of affection
and respect. What Marty *really* wanted was for her mother to
move back into her own home, which became impossible when
her mother gave the use of the house to a niece and her family.
What Tom wanted was to make it possible for his mother to
stay on the farm. Gigi wanted only to make her husband
happy, in return for the understanding he had always shown
her.

What Does the Person I Love Want For Himself?

It will help the decision making process if you make a genuine effort to find out what that person wants — not just what

he *says* he wants. These may be two very different things. If you automatically assume that person wants to live with you, you may be surprisingly wrong. Independence is treasured by many older people. The older person may not want to be in your home — for whatever reason — even though you are prepared to stoically accept a martyr's role — because you think that's what society expects of a "good" son or daughter, because it's what you want to do, or because it's what you want to have done for you in the future.

Unless she has a change of heart as she gets older, Flo has told her children to put her in a nursing home if that should become a necessity. She does not want them to miss out on their children's childhoods, as she missed out. Tom's mother, who did not recognize her physical and mental problems, wanted to stay on the farm. On the other hand, Marty's mother recognized her problem and was afraid of it. She wanted to get rid of her own house and live, permanently, with Marty and John, at all costs.

What Does the Person I Love Really Need? What Will He Need in the Future?

Everyone wants and needs to be understood. And it is important, for both you and your loved one, that you understand his condition or problem, as well as the short-term and long-term effects it will have on him and on you and your family. Is your loved one's problem physical, mental or emotional? Or is it a combination? If it is a physical problem, is the person still able to feed himself, dress himself, and go to the bathroom or is he totally dependent on other people? If it is a mental or emotional problem does he need only an occasional checking on, or does he need full-time supervision? What do you expect his physical or mental condition to be in one year? Five years? Ten years? And what do you expect your own situation and that of your family to be in one year? Five years? Ten years? Think carefully about answers to these questions.

What Do I Need?

When considering needs, be sure to consider your needs and the needs of your family, as well as those of the person you care for. Do you need peace of mind? Privacy for you and your family? Relief from the constant care of another person? Physical or emotional support? Financial assistance?

Once you determine, to your own satisfaction, what you, your family and your loved one want and need, balance these wants and needs against each other in the context of the capabilities that you and your family have for coping with the situation. Only then can you answer with confidence the following question.

What Can I Realistically Do — Financially, Physically, and Emotionally?

Finances are a very real and present concern for many people faced with this situation. Depending on the physical and emotional condition of the person involved, all of his resources and those of his family could be wiped out by a relatively short-term, critical illness or could be completely drained by a long-term chronic illness. When faced with either of these situations, it is important to put into perspective your obligation to yourself and your family as well as your obligation to that person.

While Tom, Martin, and Pat could, realistically, make arrangements to finance the care of their parents — mainly from the parent's own resources — not everyone in this book was so fortunate. Flo, the mother of two young children, was a domestic worker whose husband became unemployable because of failing health. Flo didn't even have a washer or dryer, which became for her a necessity rather than luxury. Marty's mother had invested wisely over the years, but, in these times of soaring health care costs and with her ongoing health problems, the money would not have stretched too far. Marty and John were concerned about having to contribute to her mother's care, if Marty could no longer deal with her. As it was, John was working two jobs. When John lost his regular second job and Marty cut back on her teaching, further strain was put on both family and finances.

What financial resources does your loved one have? Given current conditions and circumstances, how long is your loved one likely to live and at what level and cost of care? Will a long and lingering illness make it necessary for you to contribute financially to his care? In the not-too-distant past, children were legally responsible for the financial care of their aging parents. What if this, once again, becomes a legal responsibility? How can you plan now to see that your loved one will get the care he needs both now and for the rest of his days?

With many, if not most, people, the realities of the financial situation receive major consideration when decisions about care are being made. But there are other factors that are as important — and in some cases even more important. Too often, family members pay little attention to the physical and emotional needs of those involved — their own, as well as those of the older person.

Can you physically care for your loved one in his home or in yours? Can you, over time, continue to take care of all of the physical needs your loved one has, without sacrificing your own health or wellbeing? If that person's physical condition changes drastically, it may be necessary for the good of all concerned for you to make other arrangements for his care. Will you be willing and able to do this?

Flo paid a terrible physical price, caring for her mother-in-law during the last few years of the woman's life. Only as the result of a strong recommendation from her mother-in-law's physician did Flo and her husband agree to have his mother transferred from the hospital to a nursing home. And that, only for the last few days of her life.

Although Martin managed, rather than provided, care for his mother, the time and energy he spent running his father's business, as well as his own, and seeing to his mother's care was certainly a threat to the health of a man who had had serious bouts of illness. Fortunately for Martin's family, he survived — with his health intact.

Marty had the stamina — and a family of helpers — to handle the physical care of her mother, but can that last over time, as Marty gets older and the children leave home? What happens if her mother lives for many more years?

Finally, what are the emotional realities of your situation? Can you cope, on a day-to-day basis, with caring for your loved one in your home? Can you deal emotionally with the steady physical and/or mental deterioration of someone who isn't going to get well? Can your family deal with it?

Taking care of their mothers took an emotional toll on both Marty and Leah. Though Marty wanted her mother out of her house, she couldn't bring herself to do anything about it. Instead, she hoped against hope that her husband, John, would put his foot down. When that didn't happen, Marty became more and more upset, began to worry about the possiblity of parent abuse, and watched her family deteriorate. She had the physical stamina, but does she have the emotional stamina to "go the distance" in this very difficult relationship? When Leah could no longer deal with having her mother live with her, she put her mother in a nursing home. But the emotional strain didn't end, and it probably won't end until her mother dies. Leah speaks of her mother in the past tense, but continues her regular and painful visits to her outwardly unresponsive mother.

What Impact Will My Actions Have On Those Around Me?

If you have a family, whatever action you take will have an impact on family members — positive or negative — as well as on other persons with whom you interact. If you live alone, the actions you take could have an impact not only on your friends, but also on your colleagues and on your work, since you have no one at home to share your burden.

The strongest and ever present impact, of course, comes from the decision to care for your loved one in your home. You can't get away from it. But the decison in favor of a nursing home or, for that matter, a decision in favor of managing that person's care in his own home, will also have an effect on all concerned.

Often, having a favorite grandmother or grandfather in the home is a positive experience. Marty's husband, John, remembers with fondness the years his grandfather and grandmother lived with his family — a memory that played an important role in his willingness to put up with the problems caused by his mother-in-law. Although her mother's debilitating illness was very painful for Carol and her family, her children grew in their awareness and understanding of illness and aging, and grew in appreciation of each other as well.

Many times, however, an older person living in the home has a negative effect. The effects depend on many things, in addition to basic relationships — the physical and mental condition of the older person, the size of the home, the number and age of children (if any) in the family, the family's lifestyle, the availability and dependability of help — either paid or volunteer.

The time and energy spent managing the care of a person living alone, together with a regular visiting schedule, can have a negative effect on those around you. The extra time spent not only in seeing that the person is cared for physically, but also the time and energy spent doing or arranging for household chores to be done, can take great amounts of time and energy away from your family and friends, as well as from your work. You may also find yourself taking excessive time away from yourself and your own interests.

Martin made every effort to divide his time equitably between his parents and his wife — at the risk of his own health — to the anxiety of his family. Pat and her brother were managing from afar, with the competent help of a home health agency. (Without the agency's supervision of their mother's care, the situation would have caused even more anxiety.) Her brother's family had to share him, as well as share his emotional reactions to the situation — particulary those caused by visits to his mother. For many years, Mae divided her time between her ailing husband in one city and her ailing mother in another.

There's an impact of a different kind on families who put their loved ones in a nursing home. Usually the guilt felt as a result of taking such action radiates out to other members of the family. But it seems that one of the biggest impacts is caused by the trauma of visiting a home filled with elderly people waiting to die, as someone put it — many with no relatives or caring friends. Another is the implication this has for one's own future. Even more painful, perhaps, is to regularly visit someone you love, who has turned into a person you don't even know or a person who has become a vegetable before your own eyes.

For Joan, visiting her husband's mother was a very painful weekly experience — an experience she dreaded. It was not just that their very busy weekends — both were employed — had to be scheduled around the visit to Nana, but arrangements for every family gathering had to be scheduled around her. And the visits themselves were traumatic. Joan watched the many grim-faced, unhappy people parading in and out of the home — most of them just "doing their duty." Although she tried to find reasons to avoid the weekly visits, her husband could see through them. So, in the end, Joan gave up thinking of excuses and "did her duty," fearing for the strain on her relationship with her husband. The visits, however, triggered something else in Joan. She inevitably had to ask herself the nagging question. "Are my children going to do this to me?" And, finally, Joan had to face her own mortality.

Leah found the visits to her mother painful, despite the fact that she, herself, had been on the staff of a long-term care facility. For her, the pain was seeing her mother as the living dead — eating, sleeping, and, finally, responding only to touch and only on occasion. Yet Leah was driven to fulfill her obligation as a "good" daughter. Her pain would have been eased if the nursing home staff — knowing her mother was unaware of her visits — would have given Leah "permission" to visit less frequently.

Can I Put My Loved One in a Nursing Home If the Time Comes When I Can No Longer Care For Him or Manage His Care?

Putting someone in a home — particularly someone you love — is probably one of the most difficult decisions a family member can make, even if there is no other realistic way to care for that person. In case of a parent, you are handing over, to an institution, a person who has loved, nurtured, and guided you to adulthood. Even so, the time often comes when a careful rethinking of your situation makes it clear that a nursing home is your only alternative. A nursing home may not only be the only alternative, but it may also be the best for everyone involved — including your loved one, who will be receiving needed care that you, perhaps, are no longer able to give.

Whatever your situation is and whatever decisions you might make, it's important to know up front that taking responsibility for the care of a loved one is going to be painful from time to time. It's going to be painful when old feelings are stirred up, as they were stirred up for Pat and Leah, who had some unhappy childhood memories. Even Martin found it difficult to close down his mother's apartment, and Tom still feels a twinge of pain when he hears a beautiful soprano voice. For Carol, the pain was vividly brought into focus when she diapered her mother for the first time.

But there are strong positive memories, too:

- Martin's joy at his mother's expression of love for him in front of the young attorney.
- Tom's pleasure in watching his mother hold her great grandson.
- Flo's delight in gossiping with her mother-in-law and hearing stories of a bygone era.
- Joan's warm feelings about the interaction between Nana and Joan's two sons.
- Carol's finding a new commitment in life.
- Jane's enjoyment when she and the two old gentlemen sat down to a dinner she had fixed and pretended they were in a fancy restaurant — just like old times.
- Jim's satisfaction in being able to translate his past experience into help for an older person in need.

Although there are happy times as well as painful times, the big question is how to minimize the pain for everyone involved. It begins with honestly assessing each person's needs and arriving at the best compromise solution. While there can be no perfection, it is possible to arrive at a "universe of comfort," in which most, if not all, of your loved one's needs are met, to your satisfaction and contentment. Arriving at a universe of comfort is a challenge. As with every other challenge in life, this presents an opportunity for growth.

Carol found that caring for her mother taught her and her family about the positive side of coping. Leah's two sons grew in learning how to relate to an older person. Jane had a new appreciation of friends working with friends to accomplish something that was important to them all. Marty's children grew in their understanding of their mother and of the fact that she was trying to do something that was both unrealistic and harmful.

As you go through this experience, you'll find yourself going through cycles — periods of ease and unease. Often, just when you think things are going smoothly, something happens. You'll notice, for example, that your loved one in the nursing home has bed sores, and you suspect that he may be getting substandard care. Or, the person you're caring for at home may suddenly become deeply depressed or it may become physically impossible for you to care for that person, and you want to get rid of the problem. Guilt, of course, is your first response. You berate yourself for putting your parent in the nursing home in the first place or you berate yourself for wanting to be done with the situation.

At this precise moment, it would be a good idea to look back over what has happened. Rethink the situation. Rethink the decisions you have made along the way. Don't overlook or underestimate the fact that you made the best decisions you could, in the context of the situation at the time. Recognize, too, that situations change and life circumstances change. And different decisions often have to be made. You may need not only to rethink and reassess the situation, you may also need to reassess your feelings. Have they changed over time?

If you find yourself reassesing the situation, however, it's a good thing to resist the temptation to make a rash decision or take an abrupt action, such as stepping in immediately to take the person you love out of the nursing home. If a nursing home is the problem, think about the situation in terms of the original reasons for institutionalization and in terms of the reason for selecting the facility. You could find that such an assessment reinforces, rather than invalidates, your original decision.

If it does reinforce your earlier decision, but your concerns persist, a frank discussion with the administrator of the facility may solve the problem. Such a discussion may bring to the administrator's attention a problem that he was not aware of and, in fact, you might be doing him and the facility a service. Your conversation with the administrator will accomplish something else, too. It will remind him that you want the best quality of care for your loved one and that you are, in effect, looking over his shoulder to see that it is provided. Despite your efforts in talking with the administrator or with any other members of the staff, you may come to the conclusion that your loved one must be moved to another facility. If such a move is appropriate, don't hesitate to do it. But do it with sensitivity and caring concern for the person you are uprooting.

If your discomfort over the situation is caused by disruption in your home, it's a good idea to discuss the situation with your family and with anyone else who is intimately involved. Try to find a solution together — one that everybody can live with. The older person's physician may be able to provide invaluable counsel and direction. A caring physician will be concerned not only about the well being of his patient, but also for the well being of his patient's family. Other professionals, such as social workers, may be extremely helpful to you as well. And, finally, friends who have gone through — or are going through — the same experience will be good sources of advice and support — as you will be for them and for others later on.

The key to coming through this — and you will come through it — is to consider the situation, with all of its ramifications, from the perspective of everyone involved. It's important to do this honestly and thoughtfully, with as much objectivity as is humanly possible. The goal is to find the most equitable solution for everyone, so that you can all grow from the experience, rather than go under because of the experience.

An experience of this kind will never be forgotten. Nor will the feelings, nor will the conflicts. But it is an experience that most people have been able to come to terms with, through the passing of time, through sharing with others, and through gaining new understandings of themselves, as well as of the older person.

4.

HELP *IS* AVAILABLE

"YOU THINK it's never going to happen to you, so you're not prepared when it does." "We had no idea what services were available for my mother after she had her stroke." "We didn't know where to turn to get household help for dad when he moved back into his house after leaving the rehab center."

Faced with the need to make decisions and provide care for one who can no longer care for himself, relatives or friends often have no idea where to turn or how to look for help. They don't know how to take the first steps to get the assistance they and their loved ones need. And everyone needs some kind of assistance or support, whether it be resource information, physical care services, financial or emotional support.

There are, surprisingly, a number and variety of resources available to those who know how to find, tap into, and coordinate them — resources offered by government (federal, state, and local), by institutions, by health care organizations, associations, and agencies, and by community groups, such as community mental health centers. While these resources vary from state to state, city to city, town to town, and village to village, some form of help is available and can be found. Resources range from insurance coverage to financial aid, from visiting nurse services to comprehensive home care programs, from a variety of rehabilitation services to specialized institutional care, from "Meals on Wheels" to home management programs.

Financial Assistance

Finances — or the lack of them — is often the keystone of care for an elderly person. For those who need it — and most people do — some kind of financial help or support is available. Such support ranges from direct payment for services — such as Medicare or commercial insurance reimbursement — to provision of the care itself — such as the care provided by Veterans Administration hospitals.

Whatever aid or support your person receives, it is important that you understand the eligibility requirements for, the provisions of, and the mechanisms involved in, that reimbursement or care program. When the person you are responsible for is covered by Medicare/Medicaid or by any other kind of insurance or program, be sure you know just what the coverage includes and what it doesn't include. Be familiar, too, with such aspects of coverage as the relationship of Medicare to any supplemental insurance, how and where to submit claims, where to get answers for questions, and conditions under which coverage will be terminated.

Information about Medicare can be obtained from your local Social Security office (check your telephone book) or from such publications as *Your Medicare Handbook*, available from the U.S. Government Printing Office, Washington, D.C. 20402. (This is one of many publications available from GPO, either for no charge or for a modest charge.) In the Medicare handbook, you will learn, for example, what services are covered when the patient is in a skilled nursing home, what hospice services are covered, what outpatient services are covered. If private insurance, rather than Medicare, is involved, be sure you have a copy of the most recent policy and all related documents conveniently at hand. If you need further information or clarification, call the local office of the insurance carrier (if there is one), or write to the company's national headquarters.

If the person you care for is an armed service veteran, look into eligibility for care in a Veterans Administration facility or by a VA home care program. For further information about Veterans Administration hospitals and the services they provide, call your nearest Veterans Administration office or write to the Veterans Administration, Washington, D.C. 20402. You will need to find out what documents — e.g., discharge papers — are necessary to establish eligibility. It's a good idea also to check into other armed forces-related facilities and services, such as the Navy's marine hospitals.

Persons with certain, specific physical impairments are often eligible for additional benefits or income support. Information about such benefits as supplemental security for the aged-blind or disabled can be obtained from your local or regional office of the U.S. Department of Health and Human Services or state welfare department. For information about other governmental benefits and services, look under the heading of "Aging" in the federal, state, and local listings in your telephone directory. (In smaller cities and towns, you may have to contact the organization or agency through an office in a nearby city.)

Programs and Services

If your loved one does not need institutionalization — that is, more care then he can provide for himself or more than another person can reasonably provide for him — there are many programs and services available to make life easier for you and for the person you care for. To get an idea of what's available in your community, look under "Senior Citizens" and "Home Health Care" in the yellow pages of your local telephone directory.

Among the senior citizen's listing, you will most likely find such programs and services as:

- Adult day care centers, which provide a daily activity

program for seniors who can benefit from it.
- Community centers, which provide social and service activities for those who are able to participate.
- "Meals on Wheels" — or the local equivalent — which provides home delivered meals, on a regular basis, for those who are unable to prepare their own.
- Homemaker programs that provide aides to handle shopping and household chores for those who can no longer do them, even though they can handle other activities of daily living — e.g., washing and dressing themselves, preparing meals — well enough to stay in their own homes.

Often the older person has a chronic, physical condition(s) that requires monitoring or continuing routine services — e.g., injections, blood pressure checks — or therapy — e.g., physical therapy. Most, if not all, of these services can be provided in the home on a continuing basis. There are organizations such as the Visiting Nurses Association and other home health agencies that will provide them.

If you think home health services — in your home or in the home of the older person — may work for you, discuss it with that person's physician. Find out, first, if he thinks home health care is appropriate in your situation and, if it is, will he continue to supervise the necessary care. (His willingness to continue may be an important factor in the decision.) In all likelihood, the physician will know not only the range of services available in your community, but also the reputations of the various public and private agencies there. If, however, the physician is not aware of appropriate programs and services, other sources of information are available.

Some hospitals have their own home care programs. If the person you care for has been hospitalized, talk to the hospital's discharge planner or social worker about home care programs or services offered by the institution. If it doesn't offer any, ask about programs and services available in the community. The social service staff should be able not only to tell you what is available in the community but also what services are appropriate for your loved one.

It's a good idea to ask friends and colleagues who have been there to give you recommendations. Check also with the local public health service, with your church, with community service organizations, and with family service agencies. And, finally look in the yellow pages — under "Home Health Services" — of your local telephone directory.

Look into several organizations or agencies before you make a decision. Ask questions, questions, questions. And then compare the answers. Some of the questions you will want to ask are:

- What specific services are provided?
- What is the cost of the service needed? How are charges billed and when is payment expected?
- Are such services covered by Medicare, Blue Cross/Blue Shield, commercial insurance, or government welfare programs?
- What are the tax ramifications?
- What background is required of service personnel — e.g., aides?
- What training is provided service personnel?
- Who supervises service personnel and how do they do it?
- Who do you go to for information and for answers to questions?
- Is the agency licensed and accredited? If so, by what agency and on what date? Also ask if you can see the latest survey report.

Once you have gathered all of this information, talk again with the older person's physician. Then use your own good judgment in making the necessary decisions, knowing in your heart that you are doing the very best you can.

Sometimes the older person will need more intensive care than simple monitoring or regular routine services. Sometimes, even, he may need around-the-clock care. If that is the case — and you are unable to provide that care — proceed in this situation as you would in obtaining any other home care service. Check with the same people and the same organizations. Ask the same questions.

If you are planning to care for your loved one yourself, on a 24-hour basis, consider also a program that offers respite care. Respite care will give you and your family the opportunity to take a break from the constant care of the patient. This kind of care is usually provided during the day — so that you can get away to do things that need to be done — or on weekends. Overnight care can be provided, however, so that the family caregivers can get a good night's sleep and, in some instances even, can take a vacation. Such care is provided in the home, but it can be provided in a hospital or long-term care facility through the temporary use of unoccupied beds. It is generally believed that the patient should be kept in familiar surroundings whenever possible.

Long-Term Care Facilities

Sometimes a nursing home is the only place for an older dependent person. If that is true in your case, don't feel guilty, because you are providing the proper care for your loved one. When carefully chosen, a nursing home can meet that person's needs far better than you can and, at the same time, preserve your sanity and keep your family intact.

If you are looking for a nursing home, it's important to match the kind of care your loved one needs with the levels of care provided by the nursing homes in your area. In general, there are three levels of care provided — residential, intermediate, and skilled nursing.* Some nursing homes offer all three, some offer one or two. These levels of care related to the

---

*Actual labels or names vary by area, but the service components are, basically, the same.

intensity of professional services required — e.g., services of a registered nurse, a licensed practical nurse, or a nursing aide. (Usually, the nursing home determines the level of care your dependent person will need.)

Residental care is for persons who require more supervision than they do actual physical care. Intermediate care is for persons who need some nursing care but are, generally, up and around. Skilled care is for persons who are bedridden or who otherwise require a great deal of nursing care. Not surprisingly, nursing home costs reflect the level of care provided.

It is helpful to have some guidelines for evaluation when you are looking for a nursing home. Check with your local public health agency and state and local health care organizations, as well as community groups and private senior citizen organizations in your area. Check also with your church, your union, and your employer. Many of these organizations can provide you with information about nursing homes in the area and about the services they provide. Some will provide you with checklists for what to look for when evaluating a nursing home — checklists that focus on such areas as staffing, physical plant, licensure and accreditation. Consider also the social component of care — that is, the feeling of warmth, concern, and attention focused on the individual needs of each resident. This should permeate all services provided, from food selection and serving, to activities, to bathing and toileting, to resident-staff interaction. You can learn a lot about a nursing home simply by observing. You can also learn by asking others who have had experiences with it.

When you visit a nursing home, be sure you talk with the home's administrator. Ask about the license of the institution, the administrator's license, and the institution's accreditation status. Become informed about the nursing home patient's bill of rights. Find out about all costs and financial arrangements. Be sure you are clear about what the basic cost includes. Does it include only room, board, and minimal nursing care, with additional charges for therapy, social services, supplies, laundry, etc.? Also be sure you understand, completely, what the financial arrangements are and how payment is made. For example, some nursing homes require simply monthly payments — no deposits, no guarantees — while other homes may require that a fund be set up or that the individual turn over his entire life savings in exchange for lifetime care. With regard to other financial considerations, you'll want to find out also whether the home will accept public aid patients, if this is — or could become — a financial issue. Not all homes are certified for Medicare, which means that, even if the person qualifies for such coverage, his care will not be paid for as long as he is in an uncertified facility.

When investigating nursing homes, use the same procedures and talk to the same people suggested earlier for home care programs. Only when you have found out as much as you possibly can, about the home or homes you are considering, will you be able to make an appropriate decision — one that you can live with comfortably over time, or until it is appropriate to make a change.

Support Groups and Organizations

In addition to the groups and organizations already discussed, there are others that provide not only information, but also give support for family members of the elderly ill. The Alzheimer's Disease and Related Disorders Association, Inc. — a national organization — for example, has local chapters, which sponsor support groups and provide informational and educational materials. The organization's national headquarters are in Chicago, Illinois and it has a registered Lobbyist in Washington, D.C.

Other disease-related organizations provide varying degrees of information and service. Among them are the American Cancer Society, the American Heart Association and the American Diabetes Association. In addition to disease-related organizations, there are organizations of or for the older persons themselves. These include the American Association of Retired Persons, National Council on Aging, Grey Panthers, and many others. Among the programs and services offered by such organizations are lobbying activities, information and voluntary standard-setting.

The local chapters of many of the organizations mentioned here may be aware of other local organizations and watchdog groups that can be of assistance to you as you assess available resources in your area.

Finally, your local librarian can provide you with disease-specific literature — books and articles — as well as general literature on illness and aging. And last, but far from least, professional people — e.g., social workers and experts on aging, as well as people who have gone through the experience of caring for an older person, can be invaluable resources in your search for the most viable solution for your older loved one.

5.

. . . . BECAUSE YOU'VE BEEN THERE

IT'S HARD TO READ these stories without asking the inevitable question, "What's going to happen to me?"

Tom, Carol, Flo, Joan, and Gigi asked themselves that. Each with different results. Tom felt that he would need to follow his children's "advice," when the time came that it was offered, or have a decision foisted upon him later on. In any case, he was already planning how he would behave and survive in a nursing home. Carol felt very comfortable that her children would care for her and her husband. On the basis of her experience, Flo opted for a nursing home, rather than to disrupt her children's lives. Joan wasn't really sure what her children would do, but she *was sure* that she didn't *ever* want to go to a home. Trying to avoid the possibility of a home, at all cost, Joan made a pact with a friend that they would be bag ladies together. Gigi's thoughts went in an entirely different direction. She wanted to do things that would make her like herself — wanted to make others happy, so she would feel better, feel like she had accomplished something.

Other thoughts and questions crowded the minds of the people in this book. Joan faced her own mortality. Leah contemplated the quality of her life down the road. Questions come to mind in rapid succession. Who will be making what kinds of decisions for me and at what point in my life? What arrangements can I make for my own future? What have other people done?

Royce and Martin had inadvertently built a network of younger people that cared for them at the end of their lives. Edna also had one. But such networks are not always possible. Creating a broader living unit could help you maintain your lifestyle and continue to provide friendship and support as life inevitably takes its toll. If you, as husband and wife, have good friends — and are so inclined — a pooling of personal and emotional resources may be something to consider. Depending on the situation, financial commitments could also be made, thus improving on the lifestyle each couple would have had independently. In other situations, persons who are alone can come together in various types of arrangements to stretch their dollars and to give and gain physical and/or emotional support, as well as to diminish the fear of being sick and alone.

Other alternatives for private arrangements are also possible. In fact, some services exist, and others are developing, that can help you meet your individual needs, whether it be for housing, for assistance with activities of daily living, or for companionship, through an exchange with another person. Carefully screened and monitored, such reciprocal arrangements can meet the needs of all involved. If, for example, you need help in meal preparation and dressing, and a compatible person needs living arrangements, which you can provide, a match may just be possible. For some, this slightly more formal and supervised arrangement may result in the maintenance of independence.

In addition to such personally designed arrangements, other more formal and comprehensive ones can be made — ones that are appropriate to your physical condition and stage of life. These can include retirement complexes or villages, retirement hotels, and lifecare contracts. Such changes in living arrangements are as natural as those that take place in other stages of life. The move to larger quarters as your family grows. The move away from home by a teenager or young adult. The move to smaller quarters when your children have all gone away.

For many people, self-determination — as well as independence — have high priority in their lives, particularly as they grow older. Since we do not know what the future holds, we can only thoughtfully consider the way we would like our lives to be, given changes that inevitably occur over the years — physical impairment, illness, loss of a spouse.

If you are concerned over the possible loss of self-determination, if you are worried about who may be making decisions for you later in life, there are certain steps you can take right now. You can, for example, designate the person or persons you want to become the guardian of your estate and/or your person, should that ever become necessary.

In doing so, you will have assurance that your future will be in the hands of someone you respect and trust, someone who shares your values and knows and understands your wishes. For financial security, you can establish, for example, a trust fund, specifying in detail when and how the money is to be used. You can establish a living will, stipulating that no heroics be used, should your life become meaningless and you are simply being kept alive by machines. Whatever plans you want to make, you would be well advised to consult an attorney who can explain your options and guide your decisions, which should result in peace of mind for yourself and for those around you.

It is helpful — in fact vitally important — to discuss any such plans or arrangements with persons closest to you. Unfortunately, such conversations are difficult. Often, they don't even take place, or, if they do, they are inhibited and incomplete. Flo wanted to discuss the future with her family, but they didn't want to talk about it.

Many changes have taken place in health care delivery and financing in recent years. And more are sure to come. Who knows what the research and technological advancements will have in store for us, with regard to prolonging life, improving health, and enhancing the quality of life. One such technological advancement, for example, provides peace of mind for persons living alone. Its an electronic device that, when worn by the older person, monitors his movement, signaling, as appropriate, to the program base, where trained staff take predetermined actions. Who knows, too, what new opportunities — business or otherwise — and new discoveries will change the options that we now have relative to the quality of life as we get older. The hip replacement, for example, has given untold numbers of people a whole new lease on life.

This is not a chapter of pessimism, but one of optimism — one of identifying and utilizing a "window of opportunity." By thinking, discussing, and planning, we can improve the quality of our lives as we get older. We can learn from those who have gone this way before us. Their experiences can help us make our own lives the very best they can be, given the circumstances in which we find ourselves.

To us all . . . "L' Chiam"

To life!